THE MEXICAN WAR DIARY OF THOMAS D. TENNERY

Thomas D. Tennery about 1880

The Mexican War Diary of Thomas D. Tennery

EDITED AND WITH AN INTRODUCTION BY

D. E. Livingston-Little

UNIVERSITY OF OKLAHOMA PRESS : *Norman*

ALSO BY D. E. LIVINGSTON-LITTLE

An Economic History of North Idaho, 1800–1900 (Los Angeles, 1965)

International Standard Book Number: 0–8061–0883–5
Library of Congress Catalog Card Number: 79–88143

 Composed and printed at Norman, Oklahoma, U.S.A., by the University of Oklahoma Press. First edition.

Acknowledgments

AN expression of appreciation is due a number of people who assisted me in preparing Thomas D. Tennery's diary for publication. Tennery's great-granddaughter, Mrs. Marian Craig, secretary to the President of Los Angeles Valley College, not only provided the diary itself but did most of the work of typing and proofreading and helped secure the approval of members of the family for its publication. Others who helped were William K. Alderfer, state historian of the Illinois State Historical Library, and Theodore J. Cassady, assistant state archivist of the Illinois State Archives.

For providing the photographs of the officers and the maps, a word of thanks goes to Colonel H. A. Schmidt, chief, Historical Services Division, Office of Military History, Department of the Army; to Georgette M. Dorn, reference librarian, Hispanic Foundation, Library of Congress; and to the staff of the National Archives and Record Service. Robert V. Williams, microfilm librarian, and Miss Carroll Hart, director of the Department of Archives and History of the state of Georgia, helped me with the history of the Georgia Regiment.

Many others offered advice and guidance, among them Joe B. Frantz, of the University of Texas and the Texas State Historical Association; Fernando Barrenechea, who has offices in Nuevo Laredo, Tampico, and Veracruz, Mexico; and C. C. Stewart, chairman of the Cameron County Historical Survey Committee, Brownsville, Texas.

Lorrin Morrison, editor and publisher of the *Journal of the West*, deserves my gratitude for reasons too numerous to list. My nephew, Duane Little, put his engineering skill to work on one of the maps. Colonel Charles W. Burtyk, Jr., acting chief, Magazine and Book Division, Directorate for Defense Information, Office of the Secretary of Defense, was helpful in locating biographical data, maps, and photographs.

D. E. LIVINGSTON-LITTLE

Sherman Oaks, California
January, 1970

Editor's Introduction

RARELY, if ever, are wars popular with the American people. Most historians would agree that not much more than a third of the colonists actively supported the American Revolution. In 1812 the people of the entire northeastern section of the country so violently opposed the war that they virtually refused to contribute troops or buy bonds, and in fact met in convention at Albany, New York, to consider secession. Little testimony need be offered regarding the fratricidal Civil War. Despite bitterness on both sides there was an unparalleled rate of desertion—about a million men on each side—and in 1864 Lincoln narrowly won re-election against a peace candidate only because of timely victories at Mobile Bay and Atlanta, Georgia.

The Mexican War, from 1846 to 1848, was no exception. The antislavery forces of the North castigated President Polk and his administration, as did Whig party supporters everywhere. In fact, though the Whigs won the subsequent presidential election with war hero General Zachary Taylor, they promoted the view that the Mexican War had been prosecuted by the Democrats for the sole purpose of wresting vast tracts of land from a weak and peaceful neighboring country. They ignored the provocations, the efforts of the United States to arrive at a peaceful settlement of differences, and the relatively generous peace terms finally accorded the defeated Mexicans. It is not the purpose of this book to reopen those old arguments, but rather to present a new and different look at that war, as seen and recorded by a participant, Thomas Douthit Tennery, of Illinois.

Tennery was born in Greenup County, Kentucky, on December 22, 1819, the son of Thomas and Jane (Wilson) Tennery, both of eastern Tennessee. When Thomas was a boy, his family moved to the vicinity of Paris, Illinois, and in 1845 to Jasper County, where his father laid out the town of Granville. Thomas, who received quite a good education for his time, remained with his father until about that year, when he moved to Effingham County. There he purchased undeveloped land, for which he paid $1.33 an acre. In June, 1846, still unmarried though nearly twenty-seven years old, he joined the Illinois Volunteers and went off with his friends and neighbors to fight in the Mexican War.

During his year of service Tennery faithfully kept a diary. As the reader may judge, it is unusually well written, with some passages of considerable charm and feeling expressed in the rather romantic style of the period. He displayed a power of observation and a sympathy for his fellow men that is rare in a work of this kind.

Sometime before he died in 1891, Tennery gave the diary to his son-in-law, the Reverend John S. Cook, M.D., pastor of the Universalist Church of Leroy, Illinois. Dr. Cook made what is obviously an extremely careful and accurate typescript of the approximately two hundred pages of the longhand account and presented copies to members of the family. The whereabouts of the original journal is unknown. The diary that appears in the following pages is a reproduction of Dr. Cook's copy, with only a few changes in punctuation and spelling and the occasional insertion of a word necessary to make the meaning clear. The few missing portions were torn out of the typescript or were otherwise illegible.

I feel confident that the reader will find in Tennery's words a unique view of the Mexican War, that almost forgotten conflict whose outcome confirmed to the United States a third of its present territory.

Because so little has been published about the war in recent years, a brief account is offered for those who wish to review the circumstances that led to the conflict.

The causes of the Mexican War can be traced to the treaty by which the United States purchased the Louisiana Territory from Napoleon in 1803. The newly acquired territory was generally understood to extend from the Mississippi River to the summit of the Rocky Mountains and from the Gulf of Mexico to the Great Lakes. The northern boundary west of the Great Lakes proved too ill-defined and had to be delineated in a treaty with England, signed in 1818. The southern boundary west of the present state of Louisiana proved even harder to agree upon, for both the United States and Spain claimed Texas. In fact, at the time of the 1803 treaty the American minister to France, Robert R. Livingston, asked the French foreign minister whether the Louisiana purchase included Texas. The answer was equivocal. Livingston was in effect reminded that the United States had just made the greatest real estate bargain in history and ought not to quibble. The claims of the United States and Spain were not settled until the Florida Purchase treaty of 1819, in which Spain surrendered whatever claims she had to Oregon Territory in exchange for the surrender of whatever claims the United States had to Texas. Actually Spain gained nothing from the concession, for in 1821 she lost all of Mexico, including Texas, when that country achieved its independence.

In 1824 the United States recognized the independence of Mexico and reaffirmed the validity of the treaty of 1819 with Spain, thus conceding that Texas belonged to the Republic of Mexico. Though boundaries were not an issue at that time, Texas was regarded by both countries as extending from the Sabine River to the Río Grande.

The extremely sparse population in that frontier area soon became a matter of concern to the Mexican government, and very liberal inducements in the form of land grants were offered to attract settlers. Considerable numbers of French and especially German colonists responded, but the preponderant numbers were Americans who simply moved farther west and south from the frontier areas of the United States. Within a decade Texas had acquired a large population, mostly Americans, who were faced with the necessity of accepting Mexican citizenship, the Roman Catholic faith, and later the abolition of slavery. It is natural to have some reservations about the sincerity with which the settlers accepted those conditions. Nevertheless, they began to participate actively in the government of Mexico, then organized under the federalist constitution of 1824, which allowed a degree of local autonomy. It was not until eleven years later, when a centralist constitution deprived the Mexican states of their sovereignty, that the Texans rebelled.

Under the new constitution Texas was no longer a state of Mexico but was joined with Coahuila in a department governed like the others by President Santa Anna. The Texans' resistance to the loss of self-government brought Santa Anna himself at the head of an army to punish the rebels. Severe measures at the Alamo and at Goliad served only to arouse the Texans, who under Sam Houston met and decisively defeated the Mexican army at San Jacinto in April, 1836. Santa Anna was taken prisoner and was obliged to sign a treaty according Texas its independence—and incidentally confirming the Río Grande as the southern boundary of Texas. Santa Anna's successors in the office of president did not recognize the independence of Texas, however, repudiating both him and the treaty he had signed.

Shortly after winning its freedom, Texas applied for admission to the United States. The mere proposal to introduce such a measure in Congress caused such a furor that President Van Buren persuaded the Texans to withdraw their application. The abolitionists were beginning to enjoy some political success in their opposition to slavery. Although a decided minority, they often held the balance of power between Whigs and Democrats. They repeatedly delayed the organization of Congress and decisively influenced the presidential election of 1840. The suggestion to admit a new and large slave state aroused their violent opposition.

The admission of Texas was not seriously proposed again until 1844, when Polk made it a part of his presidential campaign platform, along with the acquisition of Oregon. By that time the belief that it was the manifest destiny of the United States to spread across the continent had gained currency. In addition, the idea of adding both a large northern and presumably free territory along with slaveholding Texas assured the support of the majority of American voters, as evidenced by Polk's victory in the election. Meanwhile, Tyler, the incumbent lame-duck president, without a party and without prospects of a political future, determined to anticipate Polk. He influenced Congress to pass a joint resolution calling for the admission of Texas.

The resolution was passed early in March, 1845, and before the year's end Texas had joined the Union.

The territorial conflicts and settlements were accompanied by oftentimes frustrating diplomatic relations between the United States and Mexico. In 1825 the diplomat Joel Roberts Poinsett became the first American minister to Mexico. He was well qualified for the position and was expected to promote cordial relations between the two countries. There was potential good will to build on. The United States had been the first nation to recognize Mexican independence, and the Mexican constitution of 1824 had been patterned on that of its northern neighbor. Poinsett soon discovered, however, that he was a Protestant in a Roman Catholic country, a democrat in a nation ruled by aristocrats, and an American in a land where the dominant foreign power was England.

Poinsett had a specific diplomatic mission to fulfill, that of negotiating a new Texas boundary treaty—if possible, one that would provide for the purchase of at least some of Texas from Mexico—and also negotiating a treaty of amity and commerce. Unfortunately, Poinsett became involved in Mexican party politics, with the result that he offended nearly everyone. He was recalled in 1829, to be replaced by Anthony Butler, a protégé of President Jackson. Poorly qualified for the post, Butler immediately aroused Mexican suspicions by visiting Texas en route to Mexico, and not until 1832 was he able to achieve a treaty of amity and commerce and one which merely reaffirmed the Texas boundaries of 1819. He failed to acquire any of Texas by purchase.

Another problem Butler faced was the growing number of American claims against Mexico arising out of the destruction, theft, or confiscation of American property in

Mexico and the robbery, mistreatment, imprisonment, and even murder of Americans in Mexico. Years were spent in futile efforts to obtain redress. In 1843 some compensation was finally made, in compliance with the findings of an international arbitration committee. In the meantime, Butler had been recalled in 1835, only months before Mexico lost Texas.

The end of the first decade of diplomatic relations between the United States and Mexico thus found the two countries estranged and antagonistic. The United States, though frustrated in its efforts to buy any part of Texas, widely criticized in the Mexican press, and almost powerless to protect American citizens from mistreatment—oftentimes by officers of the Mexican government—continued its efforts to reach an accord with its southern neighbor. Mexico, on the other hand, nurturing grievances fancied and real (including Butler's conduct), showed nothing but hostility toward the United States. That was the situation in early 1836, when Texas won its independence and almost immediately applied for admission to the United States. The Mexicans, convinced that their worst suspicions had been realized, warned the United States government that Texas was still Mexican territory and that its admission to the Union would be regarded as just cause for a declaration of war.

In the same year the Mexican government enacted a law prohibiting foreigners from settling in Mexican border states, a direct violation of the commercial treaty of 1832 with the United States. In 1840 a group of Americans were arrested in California under the law and sent to Tepic, and were later released only at the insistence of the British minister. Several American newspaper correspondents and merchants accompanying the 1841 Texas expedition to

Santa Fe were arrested and imprisoned in Mexico for nearly a year. In 1843, Santa Anna not only closed the border to trade with the United States (particularly the Santa Fe–Chihuahua trade) but soon thereafter barred the import of a long list of articles that made up virtually the entire United States trade with Mexico. In response to a protest lodged by the American secretary of state to this new violation of the treaty, Mexico went even further and prohibited aliens from doing any retail trade in Mexico. In the same year the governors of the northern border provinces were ordered to expel all American citizens. Early in 1844, after Waddy Thompson, the American minister to Mexico, demanded his passport, the order was modified.

By that time relations between the countries could scarcely have been worse, and when the proposal to admit Texas to the Union was brought up again, Juan Almonte, the Mexican minister in Washington, threatened to break off relations. In an effort to placate the Mexican government, Thompson was authorized to offer a cash award or gift to persuade Mexico to settle the outstanding difficulties, especially that of the Texas boundary. Santa Anna's response was again to threaten war. In October, 1844, Secretary of State John C. Calhoun defended Texas' right to act as an independent nation but renewed the offer of a liberal settlement of all outstanding disputes. The Mexican foreign minister replied by repeating and expanding on all the old complaints, further worsening feeling between the countries. In early March, 1845, when President Tyler signed the joint declaration of Congress calling for admission of Texas, Almonte protested and, despite a conciliatory reply by James Buchanan, Polk's secretary of state, broke off diplomatic relations and returned to Mexico.

Polk immediately sought to re-establish relations by sending a confidential agent, William S. Parrott, to Mexico to ask the Mexican government whether it would receive an American envoy. President José Herrera appeared willing to do so, and Polk appointed John Slidell of Louisiana as United States commissioner to Mexico. Unfortunately, by the time Slidell landed at Veracruz in November, 1845, the Herrera regime had lost power, and the members of the Mexican Council of State maintained that the United States was trying to trap them into accepting a minister. Mariano Paredes, who took over the presidency in December, refused to receive Slidell and on January 4, 1846, vowed to defend Texas to the Sabine River. At this point it is sufficient to add only that for the next two years Polk never gave up trying to settle the conflict through diplomatic means.

Perhaps because relations with Mexico had been poor for many years without erupting into open conflict, the American government did not make any real plans for a war until fighting actually began. The immediate cause of hostilities was, of course, the admission of Texas, and more specifically the dispatching of United States armed forces to the new American border on the Río Grande. As the formal admission of Texas approached in mid-1845, Polk alerted Colonel Zachary Taylor to assemble his troops at a port of embarkation. Taylor, who had been breveted brigadier general for his defeat of the Seminoles in Florida in 1837, was the military commander of the Southwest and was stationed at Fort Jesup, in western Louisiana. At the fort he assembled about 1,500 of the 7,200 men then constituting the United States Army, and in June, 1845, he moved them to New Orleans. There he received further orders from Secretary of War William L. Marcy to ship the men to Texas and hold them at some point on or near the

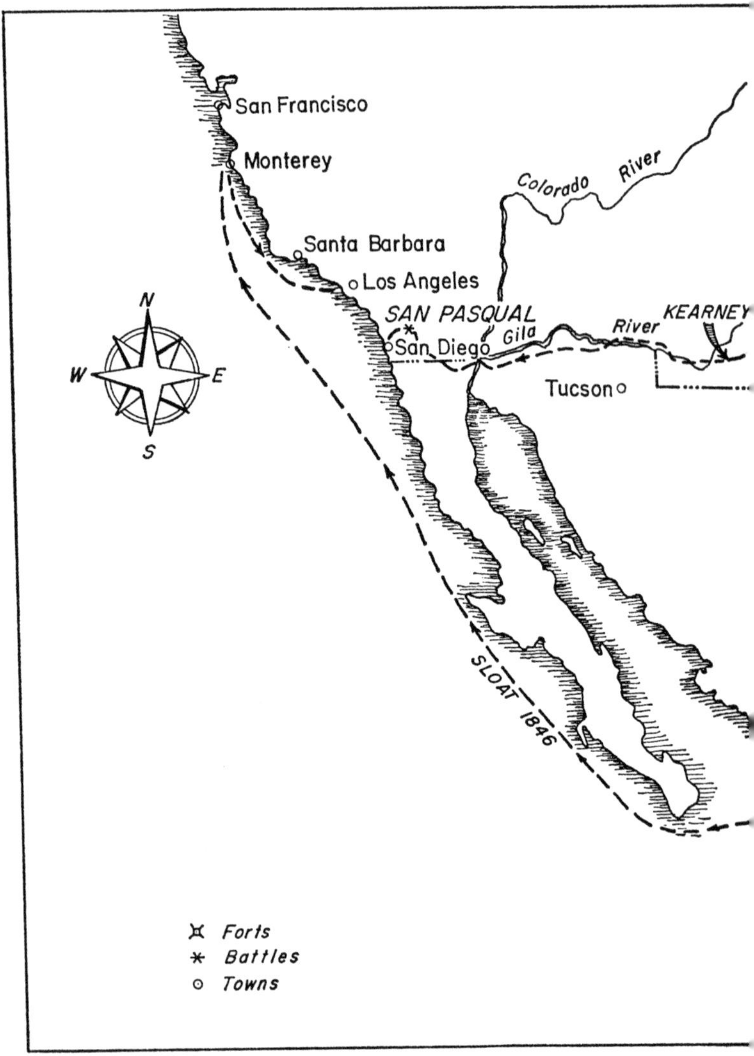
San Francisco
Monterey
Colorado River
Santa Barbara
Los Angeles
N
W
E
S
SAN PASQUAL
San Diego
Gila River
KEARNEY
Tucson
SLOAT 1846
Forts
Battles
Towns

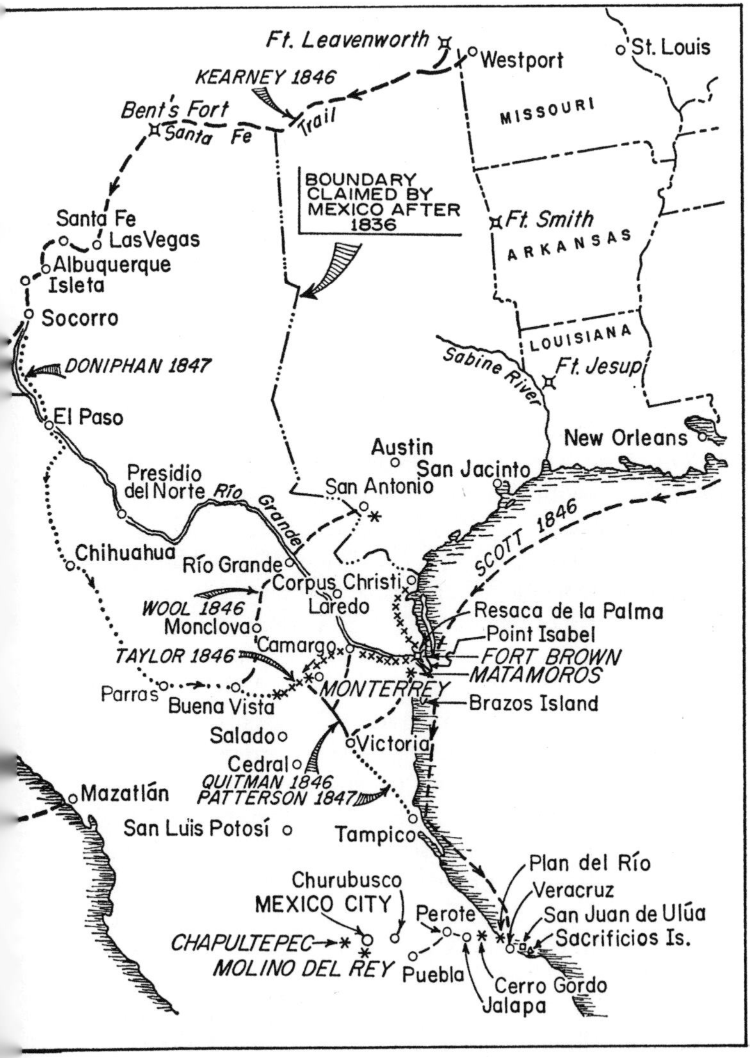
Ft. Leavenworth
Westport
St. Louis
KEARNEY 1846
Bent's Fort
Santa Fe
Trail
MISSOURI
BOUNDARY CLAIMED BY MEXICO AFTER 1836
Santa Fe
Las Vegas
Albuquerque
Isleta
Socorro
Ft. Smith
ARKANSAS
LOUISIANA
DONIPHAN 1847
Sabine River
Ft. Jesup
El Paso
New Orleans
Austin
San Jacinto
Presidio del Norte
Río Grande
San Antonio
SCOTT 1846
Chihuahua
Río Grande
Corpus Christi
Laredo
WOOL 1846
Monclova
Resaca de la Palma
Point Isabel
Camargo
TAYLOR 1846
FORT BROWN
MATAMOROS
MONTERREY
Parras
Buena Vista
Brazos Island
Salado
Victoria
Cedral
QUITMAN 1846
PATTERSON 1847
Mazatlán
San Luis Potosí
Tampico
Plan del Río
Churubusco
Veracruz
MEXICO CITY
Perote
San Juan de Ulúa
CHAPULTEPEC
Sacrificios Is.
MOLINO DEL REY
Puebla
Cerro Gordo
Jalapa

Río Grande but to avoid aggression and not to disturb any Mexican posts that he might find on the north bank of the river "unless an actual state of war should exist."

Taylor landed the troops near Corpus Christi, on the south bank of the Nueces River, which Mexico sometimes claimed constituted the southern boundary of Texas. Taylor remained there while Slidell waited in Jalapa, above Veracruz, to be received by the Mexican government. When Polk learned of the rejection of Slidell in January, 1846, he ordered Taylor to move to the Río Grande, though he again cautioned the general not to provoke a conflict. By March 20, Taylor had covered the two hundred miles to the Río Grande and was camped opposite Matamoros, where he began construction of Fort Brown.

On April 11, General Pedro de Ampudia arrived at Matamoros with about three thousand reinforcements and assumed command of the Mexican forces, including those of General Francisco Mejía, the commander at Matamoros. Ampudia demanded that Taylor withdraw his army to a position north of the Nueces River. Taylor's response was to have United States naval forces blockade the mouth of the Río Grande. On April 24 yet another Mexican general, Mariano Arista, took command of the Mexican army, with orders to attack the Americans. Arista ordered his cavalry general, Anastasio Torrejón, to cross the Río Grande above Matamoros with about sixteen hundred troops. Taylor learned of the move and sent Captain Seth B. Thornton with sixty dragoons upriver to reconnoiter. They were ambushed the next day, Thornton was captured, and all his men were killed or taken prisoner. Both Arista and Taylor announced that hostilities had begun.

In Washington, Polk, who had at last despaired of a peaceful solution to the conflict, had about decided to inform Congress of the imminence of war. News of the attack on Thornton reached Washington on May 9, and on May 11 the President delivered his message to Congress, asking for and receiving a declaration of war and authorization for an expenditure of ten million dollars and the recruiting of fifty thousand volunteers. Despite the opposition of Whig leaders, the vote for war was overwhelming: 174 to 14 in the House and 40 to 2 in the Senate. The decision to go to war was made easier by the fact that a treaty settling the Oregon question had just been signed with Britain.

The time for plans and decisions had indeed arrived. Half of the fifty thousand volunteers, all infantrymen, were to be drawn from the populous northeastern section of the country; slightly fewer were to be requested of the southern and western states. The remaining forces, bringing the total to the authorized number, had already been called out by the governors of Texas and Louisiana at Taylor's request. About one-third of the southern and western units were to be cavalry. In addition, the regular army was increased to about seventeen thousand, mostly by increasing the size of each company from sixty-four to one hundred privates. The navy was also increased, both in manpower and in ships.

It was left up to the individual states to work out details for recruiting the volunteers. Some of the states utilized existing militia organizations, which were filled to strength or expanded as necessary. Most of the officers were elected by the men who served under them, a practice commendable in its democracy but scarcely conducive to effective discipline, as would be evident in the months to come.

Having provided for the tools of war, the government next laid plans for their employment. The war strategy was based on the assumption that all the people of northern Mexico were ripe for rebellion against a central government that had historically done little to deserve their loyalty or gratitude. The territories of New Mexico and California especially seemed so alienated that it was a matter of some concern to the United States that a European power, such as Britain or France, might move in. Polk, like other leaders before him, hoped to add to United States territory not only Texas but, if possible, New Mexico and California as well. Those assumptions and concerns were apparent in the American war strategy and tactics.

The only battle orders issued before the declaration of war were the tentative and provisional ones sent to Commodore John D. Sloat, commander of the Pacific Squadron, late in 1845. Sloat had been instructed that if actual hostilities broke out he was to seize California from Mexico. During a call at the port of Mazatlán, Mexico, early in June, 1846, Sloat became suspicious that fighting was indeed under way, and, determined to anticipate a possible landing by British naval forces, he sailed to Monterey, California, which he occupied peacefully on July 7. A subordinate occupied the port of San Francisco a few days later, also without bloodshed.

Commodore Robert F. Stockton, who succeeded Sloat in July, swore in John C. Frémont and other Americans as volunteers and sailed south to take Los Angeles and San Diego. At Los Angeles little more than token resistance was encountered until an overzealous marine captain, Archibald H. Gillespie, who had been left in command of a fifty-man garrison in the city, provoked the Californians to violence. After sending north to Colonel Frémont for help, the garrison was forced to withdraw to a ship in San Pedro Harbor.

In the meantime, Colonel Stephen Watts Kearny, soon to be promoted to brigadier general, had been authorized to recruit a regiment of cavalry in Missouri and to follow the Santa Fe Trail to New Mexico and take control of that territory. Then, if it proved feasible, he was to move on into California. In addition to his own 300 First Dragoons, Kearny was accompanied by the First Regiment of Missouri Mounted Volunteers (about 860 men) under Colonel Alexander W. Doniphan, two batteries of artillery, a volunteer cavalry company, and some Indian scouts—about 1,660 men in all. Lieutenant Colonel Philip St. George Cooke followed with a battalion of Mormons who were moving west to California. Kearny anticipated a desperate defense by New Mexico Governor Manuel Armijo at Santa Fe, but at the last moment the governor left the territory, and Kearny took New Mexico without resistance.

After setting up a territorial government and making some effort to pacify the Indian inhabitants (who were later to stage a bloody though abortive uprising), Kearny proceeded down the Río Grande Valley. At Socorro he met Kit Carson, who carried the premature news of California's capture. Kearny sent all the troops but one hundred men back to Santa Fe to avoid leading a large force across the desert. Then, with the remaining escort, he turned west, following the Gila River to the Colorado.

Late in November Kearny and the escort crossed the Colorado and entered California. Before he and his men had had time to recover from the ordeal of crossing the desert, they were attacked by a troop of California lancers at San Pasqual and suffered heavy casualties. Relieved by Commodore Stockton, who was nearby at San Diego, the survivors joined forces with Stockton's men and moved north to Los Angeles, which was recaptured after a brief battle. Frémont, who arrived almost simultaneously from the north, accepted the surrender of the Californians at Rancho Cahuenga, near Los Angeles, early in January, 1847, and the struggle for California was ended.

Colonel Doniphan and his Missouri Mounted Volunteers were among those left in New Mexico when Kearny moved on to California. Anticipating that Doniphan's men would not be needed long in New Mexico, Kearny offered them to General John E. Wool for a proposed attack on Chihuahua. It was not until December, 1846, that circumstances combined to free Doniphan for his move southward. By that time twelve hundred additional troops had arrived from Missouri, as well as the Mormon battalion, and the Indians had been pacified.

Meanwhile, about three hundred traders with a large wagon train of merchandise were waiting in southern New Mexico, afraid to proceed toward Chihuahua because of a Mexican military force sitting astride their trail at El Paso. On December 12, Doniphan set out, picking up the caravan, and advanced on El Paso. Upon receiving confirmation that a large Mexican army with artillery was assembled at El Paso, he sent back a request for an artillery battery but moved forward without waiting for it to catch up with him. At El Brazito, about thirty miles from El Paso, he met the Mexican army and in a forty-minute skirmish inflicted heavy casualties, with only small losses to his own men (seven wounded), and put the Mexicans to flight.

At El Paso, where his regiment was warmly received, Doniphan waited for the arrival of the artillery battery, under the command of Major Meriwether Lewis Clark. Upon learning that General Wool was not going to Chihuahua, Doniphan set out on his own, leaving El Paso on February 8, 1847. He led a total force of thirteen to fourteen hundred men, having organized and sworn in the wagon train's traders and teamsters as a battalion, under the command of Samuel C. Owens, a trader from Independence, Missouri. Encountering little opposition other than that resulting from weather and geography, the Americans were within a day's march of Chihuahua before they met the Mexican forces assembled to defend the city. Three to four thousand Mexicans had gathered and fortified a point where the El Paso road crossed the Río Sacramento. Although the Battle of Sacramento lasted most of the day, Doniphan lost only one man killed (Major Clark) and a half dozen wounded. The Mexican forces suffered several hundred casualties and finally scattered and disbanded. The American army occupied Chihuahua the following day, March 1.

Doniphan's command remained at or near Chihuahua until April 27, by which time messengers had reached General Wool in Saltillo with news of the town's capture. Since most of the wagon train of merchandise had been disposed of by then, and since his men's terms of enlistment would expire in another month, Doniphan marched his forces to Saltillo, arriving there on May 21. Moving quickly to Monterrey, which had fallen to General Taylor (see below) and then to the Río Grande, Doniphan's men took ship for New Orleans and traveled up the Mississippi to Missouri.

The change in strategy had been dictated by circumstances. In June, 1846, General Wool, then stationed in Louisville, Kentucky, had been directed to take command of troops under orders to assemble at San Antonio for the proposed expedition to Chihuahua. Wool traveled down the Ohio and the Mississippi, reaching New Orleans toward the end of July. He took ship and sailed to the Texas coast and moved inland, arriving in San Antonio in mid-August (Tennery's regiment traveled on the same boat with Wool down the Mississippi and sailed with him to Texas).

There he undertook to bring order out of chaos and on September 25 finally moved south with the first contingent of about fourteen hundred men. After marching nearly two hundred miles, he crossed the Río Grande near Presidio de Río Grande and camped just beyond the town to rest for a week. During that week Wool's forces were augmented by the arrival of Brigadier General James Shields with about six hundred men of the First Illinois Volunteers. Shields also brought news of Taylor's victory at Monterrey.

Moving on toward Monclova, Wool and Shields reached Santa Rosa on October 24, and, despite the threatening presence of a Mexican force of twenty-five hundred mounted irregulars, Monclova was taken without a battle on October 29. Within a week Colonel Sylvester Churchill arrived with twelve hundred men, the remaining group of Illinois Infantry and two or three companies of cavalry, his force constituting the rear section of the expedition. Forced to wait in Monclova for a month because of Taylor's armistice commitments (see below), Wool finally received orders to abandon plans for the Chihuahua expedition and instead move south to Parras, just west of Saltillo. General Shields and Colonel William S. Harney were detached from Wool's command and ordered back to the Río Grande.

On November 24, Wool began the 180-mile march to Parras, where he arrived on December 5. After about two weeks there, he was ordered to join General William J. Worth, south of Saltillo, and did so on December 17. His troops had marched 900 miles, 700 of them through enemy territory, without firing a shot. In the process they had developed into a trained and disciplined force.

In the meantime General Taylor had been engaged in securing the eastern coastline. When Captain Thornton was captured on the Río Grande in May, 1846, the total

Mexican force under Arista at Matamoros probably numbered about five thousand, divided into two brigades of infantry and one of cavalry, with artillery support for each. Near the site of the upper ferry at Anaquitas, the Mexicans built Fort Paredes to command the river crossing and at two points lower down installed additional redoubts with artillery sited to converge on Fort Brown. Meanwhile, having disposed of Thornton's small force, General Torrejón moved around Fort Brown and for several days held the road to Point Isabel (opposite the northern end of Brazos Island), about ten miles north of the mouth of the Río Grande, thinking to cut off Taylor's supplies. On May 1, Torrejón was forced to abandon his position astride the road in order to meet Arista, who had moved Ampudia's infantry brigade downriver and needed assistance in crossing the river at Longoreño.

On the same day Taylor finally realized the danger of leaving Fort Brown isolated and inadequately defending Point Isabel (later called Fort Polk). Indeed, on May 6 a Mexican brigade from Matamoros under General Ampudia attacked Fort Brown, killing one American, Major Brown. With a wagon train and slightly more than two thousand men, Taylor hurried to Point Isabel, passing north of Arista's forces before they could resume the post abandoned by Torrejón. After three days at Point Isabel, Taylor's little army began the return march to Fort Brown. On the second day, near the water hole at Palo Alto, they first saw the Mexican army, which by now numbered about four thousand men. Arista advanced with his entire force spread across a wide front, a tactic that did not prevent the American artillery from inflicting heavy damage. The Mexican artillery was generally ineffective. The battle, which began at about half-past two in the afternoon, was delayed by a grass fire and finally halted at dusk. The Americans had suffered fewer than fifty casualties, including five killed; the Mexicans, perhaps three hundred.

As dawn broke on May 9, the Mexican army could be seen moving off toward Matamoros, and scouts discovered that it had taken up a new position near Resaca de la Palma, about halfway to Matamoros. General Taylor attacked the Mexicans, led by General Mejía, and despite reinforcements provided by Ampudia and Arista, the Mexicans were routed from Resaca de la Palma and retreated toward Matamoros. Taylor was unable to pursue them effectively, and most of the survivors succeeded in recrossing the river. The Mexicans had lost three to four hundred dead and wounded and about two hundred captured. Of the seventeen hundred Americans engaged in the battle, thirty-three were killed and eighty-nine wounded. Ten days later Arista withdrew the Mexican army to Linares, and Taylor's forces occupied Matamoros and laid plans for an advance on Monterrey.

Late in June the first of the volunteer regiments authorized by Congress reached the Río Grande, and by the first of August, Taylor's army had swelled to more than twenty thousand men. They were encamped at Point Isabel, on Brazos Island, at Camp Belknap across from Burrita, on the river beyond Matamoros, and, by the end of the month, at Reynosa and Camargo, both of which had been occupied by August 1.

Camargo, on the San Juan River, three or four miles below the point at which the San Juan empties into the Río Grande, seemed a natural point for assembling troops and supplies for the expedition to Monterrey. It proved to be an unwise choice, however; it was not a healthful site, and many of the fifteen thousand troops camped there succumbed to the heat or died of various maladies. Either Reynosa, about fifty miles downriver, or Mier, a few miles above Camargo on the road to Monterrey, would have been a better choice. Moreover, there seems to have been no reason to assemble such a large force there; Taylor apparently never planned to use more than half of his troops in the attack on Monterrey.

On August 19, General Worth, commanding two thousand regulars, set out for Cerralvo, sixty miles south, halfway to Monterrey. By August 25 his first brigade had reached the town, and by September 12 the rest of Taylor's army had assembled there. The army was made up of Worth's Second Division, the First Division of Regulars under General David E. Twiggs, and the Volunteer Division commanded by Major General William O. Butler. The First Brigade of Volunteers was commanded by Brigadier General Thomas L. Hamer, and the Second Brigade was led by Brigadier General John A. Quitman. Each brigade of volunteers consisted of two regiments, each with about five hundred effectives. When they left Cerralvo for Monterrey, Taylor's forces numbered about sixty-five hundred men. By September 19 the Americans were inspecting the defenses of Monterrey.

Taylor's strategy was based on recent political events. The Paredes government had been overthrown in August, and Santa Anna had been allowed to pass through the American naval blockade at Veracruz. Returned from his exile in Cuba, Santa Anna forgot his promise to Polk to negotiate a peace and instead took supreme command of the Mexican armies. General Mejía had already assembled four thousand men at Monterrey. Fourteen hundred reinforcements arrived on August 29, and about two thousand more arrived a few days later. Thus General Ampudia, who was now in command, had a force of more than seven thousand men, as well as forty cannon, to defend a well-fortified city of stone houses and outlying defenses. Actually, however, to man all the fortifications he needed a much larger force. Attacking on September 20, General Worth soon captured three of the outlying bastions and cut off the road to Saltillo. On September 23, after three days of hard fighting, Ampudia asked for terms. An eight-week armistice was signed providing that the Americans would remain behind their lines while the Mexican army evacuated Monterrey and withdrew to Saltillo. (In point of fact, Ampudia did not stop at Saltillo but on orders from Santa Anna withdrew to San Luis Potosí, some distance farther south.) The armistice agreed upon by Taylor and Ampudia was subject to the approval of their respective governments. On November 5 the United States sent notice to Santa Anna that offensive operations would be resumed on November 15.

General Robert Patterson had been left in command of the forces still encamped along the Río Grande when Taylor launched the expedition to Monterrey. Those forces included twenty-one hundred men at Camargo under Generals Gideon J. Pillow and Humphrey Marshall, eleven hundred men at Matamoros under Colonel Charles Clark, an additional forty-five hundred along the lower reaches of the river, about fourteen hundred hospitalized soldiers, and a small contingent at Point Isabel—altogether nearly ten thousand men. Sometime earlier Polk had suggested that Patterson employ a contingent of those troops to occupy Tamaulipas, the easternmost of the Mexican border states. In December, after the inevitable delays, Patterson finally set in motion two columns, one from Camargo made up of two brigades, mostly regulars, under Quitman and Twiggs, and the other from Matamoros, under Pillow, made up of the Third and Fourth Illinois and the Tennessee Cavalry regiments, all volunteers.

In the interval since Polk's suggestion to invade Tamaulipas, other and more important tactics had been worked out. Concluding that the Mexicans would not sue for peace despite the loss of their northern territories, the administration in Washington ordered Winfield Scott, the commanding general of the army, to invade Mexico at Veracruz and strike at the capital, Mexico City.

No doubt the administration was motivated in part by the public acclaim Taylor was being accorded for his victories on the battlefield and the well-justified suspicion that he would use it to advantage as a Whig candidate for president in 1848. General Scott was also a Whig, however, and despite an abortive plan to have him superseded as commander by Democratic Senator Thomas Hart Benton of Missouri, Scott was directed to take personal charge of the invasion.

Scott called upon Taylor to release to him as many troops as Taylor could spare, retaining only enough to defend the territory he already held. As events developed, Taylor kept back eight hundred regulars and between six and seven thousand seasoned volunteers, including Wool's troops. He could also count on two or three thousand more volunteers that were due to arrive in the near future. Thus it was also in compliance with the later orders that the columns from Camargo and Matamoros set out, while Taylor himself led a third force from Monterrey, which joined with Quitman's force at Montemorelos on December 16. From that point Taylor was briefly recalled by a threatened attack by Santa Anna upon Saltillo, but he rejoined the others as they met Patterson's column in Victoria, the capital of Tamaulipas.

In Taylor's absence Butler, whom Taylor had left in charge at Monterrey, received orders from Scott on January 3 to assemble a force at the mouth of the Río Grande to attack Veracruz. The force was to comprise four thousand regular infantry, four thousand volunteer infantry, five hundred regular cavalry, and five hundred of the best volunteer cavalry, plus two batteries of field artillery. Worth, who was to command the force, was authorized to deduct such numbers as were already on their way to Tampico by way of Ciudad Victoria. Taylor also received a copy of the order and complied by sending all the men from Ciudad Victoria to Tampico and started back to Monterrey with an escort on January 14, 1847. Slightly more than half of the troops requisitioned were now approaching Tampico, which had been taken on November 15 of the previous year by naval forces under Commodore David Conner and had been garrisoned with twelve hundred artillery and Louisiana volunteers. Worth promptly moved the remainder of the troops required to Brazos Island, where for lack of transport they were forced to remain for nearly a month. The troops in Tampico fared no better. Many had to wait six weeks for vessels to take them south. On February 20, Scott learned that the Lobos Islands, sixty miles south of Tampico, offered a large, safe anchorage, and he directed the six regiments in New Orleans to proceed directly there.

While Scott was gathering his troops to move against Veracruz, Santa Anna decided that the time was ripe to attack Taylor. Leaving San Luis Potosí with more than fifteen thousand soldiers, Santa Anna marched the two hundred miles to Buena Vista in twenty days. The Battle of Buena Vista was fought on February 22 and 23. It was a confused battle, fought over broken ground, and at one time or another most of the American units showed their backs to the enemy, though on each occasion they rallied. The American artillery was again highly effective, and by the end of the second day Santa Anna had concluded that he could not win a decisive victory and withdrew with the remnants of his army. Although Taylor's forces had been outnumbered by more than two to one, they had inflicted very heavy losses on the Mexican troops, of whom about 1,800 had been killed or wounded and 300 captured. Probably 4,000 soldiers had deserted. Taylor's casualties totaled 673.

As Santa Anna hurried south, he tried to portray the battle as a victory for the Mexicans, displaying as evidence captured colors and cannon. By the time his army (about half of his original force) reached San Luis Potosí, Santa Anna was being hailed throughout the country as a hero, and he was soon called upon to assume the presidency. It was now April 1, and in the meantime Scott had accepted the surrender of Veracruz on March 29. Santa Anna had little time to prepare his defenses against Scott's advance on the capital.

On March 9 more than ten thousand American troops were put ashore behind Sacrificios Island, just south of Veracruz. On March 13 they reached the shore north of Veracruz, thereby surrounding the city. Scott warned the Mexicans to expect a bombardment and probably an assault. New batteries were constructed (seven in all), and the shelling was heavy. On March 26 the defenders of the city asked to negotiate terms of surrender. Three days later both Veracruz and the fortress of San Juan de Ulúa capitulated. Despite the attacks of Mexican irregulars and the fifteen thousand rounds of cannon fired by the Mexican artillery, the Americans had lost only nineteen killed and sixty-three wounded. The rapid and inexpensive victory was extremely important to Scott, who knew that he must immediately move the main body of his army to higher altitudes to avoid an expected epidemic of yellow fever. Mexican losses had not been great; the quick surrender was the result of the effect of Scott's artillery on the Mexicans' morale. The army's heavy guns had failed to arrive in time for the siege, owing to the interruption of shipping by frequent storms. In their place naval guns and crews had been provided by Commodore Matthew C. Perry, who had succeeded to Conner's command.

Scott had two pressing problems: first, to remove his men from the lowlands before the fever-bearing mosquitoes returned and, second, to obtain enough horses, mules, and wagons to transport supplies. Reports by scouts indicated that no determined resistance would be offered by the Mexicans between Veracruz and Jalapa, about seventy-five miles inland. Jalapa was safely out of the fever zone, and it appeared that supplies, including forage, and draft animals could be obtained there. On April 8, Twiggs was ordered to Jalapa with the Second Division of Regulars. Moving out on the National Highway, Twiggs reached Plan del Río in three days, just below Cerro Gordo, where he encountered unexpectedly heavy resistance. Turned back on April 12, Twiggs was planning a counterassault on the thirteenth when Patterson arrived with the volunteer division and assumed command. On the fourteenth Scott himself reached Plan del Río and took charge.

Lieutenants Robert E. Lee and Peter G. T. Beauregard reconnoitered the Mexican position and reported that it was nearly impregnable. They estimated that the camp was manned by twelve to eighteen thousand Mexican soldiers, with cannon emplaced on all the high ridges and hills to command the National Highway. Lee and Beauregard suggested simply cutting a road around the position. Scott agreed.

The battle plan Scott devised called for the main effort to

be made on the enemy's left in such a way as to regain the highway to Jalapa behind the Mexican troops and cut off their retreat. Pillow was to attack the Mexican right, nearest to the American camp at Plan del Río, after Twiggs with five thousand men had moved toward the center, using part of his force to take the hill La Atalaya and hold it until Shields's brigade, also a part of Twiggs's command, worked its way through to the Mexican left flank.

On the first day of the battle, which began on April 17, 1847, Twiggs moved up and succeeded in taking and holding La Atalaya with his first brigade (commanded by Colonel William S. Harney, replacing Persifor F. Smith, who was ill). During the afternoon and evening the remainder of Twiggs's division moved up to the foot of La Atalaya and during the night managed to haul cannon to the top of the hill, from which the next day they shelled the next hill, El Telégrafo.

Early on the same day Twiggs's second brigade, under Shields, composed of the Third and Fourth Illinois Volunteers (the latter Tennery's regiment) and the New York Regiment, moved in that order to attack the Mexican left and regain the highway to Jalapa. While they struggled along Lee's makeshift road, hacked through two miles of dense brush, Twiggs ordered Harney to attack El Telégrafo directly from La Atalaya. Simultaneously Brevet Colonel Bennet Riley moved from the base of La Atalaya to his right and attacked El Telégrafo from almost the opposite direction. Both columns gained the summit, sending the Mexicans fleeing into the ranks of counterattacking forces rushed forward by Santa Anna. Into this confusion the Americans turned and fired a cannon from the hill they had just taken and then charged into the Mexican troops. Santa Anna had fresh regiments available, but at that moment

Shields's brigade, commanded by Colonel Edward D. Baker (Tennery's commanding officer), appeared at the Mexicans' left, and panic began to spread. As Riley's men silenced the guns that had momentarily blunted the attack of Shields's brigade, the Fourth Illinois and the New Yorkers pressed forward to the highway almost behind the Mexican camp. Seeing themselves about to be trapped, the Mexican soldiers fled, pursued by Baker's men and the cavalry almost to Jalapa.

Though successful, the well-conceived battle plan had in fact been poorly executed. Twiggs had charged forward too soon, and Pillow's attack had failed, though the commander of the Mexican right surrendered to him when he saw that he was cut off and the battle lost. Worth had held his forces in reserve and had taken no part in the fighting.

Most of the Mexicans escaped or were paroled the following day, but they could not be enticed to make another stand short of the capital. The way to Mexico City was open. If Scott had possessed a larger force and adequate supplies and transport, he might have made a successful attack on the capital. As it was, he took Jalapa and Puebla without a fight and then rested his troops. He set out in August and captured Contreras, Churubusco, and Molino del Rey. General Shields captured Chapultepec on September 13, and on the fourteenth Mexico City fell to General Worth, and American forces entered the halls of Montezuma.

Four months later, on February 2, 1848, the Treaty of Guadalupe Hidalgo was signed, confirming the Texas boundaries and conveying to the United States the territory which today makes up California, Nevada, Utah, Arizona, New Mexico, and portions of Colorado and Wyoming. The United States paid Mexico fifteen million dollars for the ceded lands and also assumed the claims of American citizens against Mexico. By the terms of the treaty Mexico lost about 1 per cent of her population—and half of her territory.

Now for a look at the Mexican War through the eyes of Thomas D. Tennery, private, Fourth Illinois Volunteers.

Contents

Acknowledgments	*page v*
Editor's Introduction	*vii*
The Mexican War Diary of Thomas D. Tennery	
1846	3
1847	52
Epilogue	99
Appendix	108
News Report from The Georgian, September 14, 1846	
Bibliography	111
Index	113

Illustrations

Thomas D. Tennery about 1880 — *Frontispiece*

Major Thomas L. Harris — *Following page* 24
Colonel Edward D. Baker
Brigadier General James Shields
Zachary Taylor
Brigadier General John Ellis Wool
Brevet Major General David E. Twiggs
Major General Winfield Scott
Major General Gideon Johnson Pillow
Colonel William Selby Harney
Brigadier General John Anthony Quitman

Major General Robert Patterson — *Following page* 72
Landing at Veracruz, March 9, 1847
Bombardment of Veracruz, March 22 and 23, 1847
Bombardment of Veracruz, view from the sea
Map of the siege of Veracruz
View of Cerro Gordo
Battle of Cerro Gordo
Thomas D. Tennery and family

MAP

The Mexican War, 1846–48 — *Pages xvi–xvii*

THE MEXICAN WAR DIARY OF THOMAS D. TENNERY

1846

June 29.—Left home and went to Shelbyville, Ill.

June 30.—Left Shelbyville in company with Levi Hite, Theophilus Johnson, James Inman, James Henry, James Perryman[1] and Samuel Cary, who volunteered his services to take us to Alton. We camped about seventeen miles southwest of Shelbyville on the Greenville road.

July 1.—On the road at sunrise, we passed today through beautiful prairie, crossing occasionally small bodies or points of timber. About eleven o'clock we fell in with one Hinton. He pressed us to stop at his house, while he prepared to go with us to see his son, who was in Captain Thomas's[2] company of Fayette County. Accordingly there are eight of us together now; we passed through Greenville this evening and camped at Captain Wiley's.[3]

[1] The six volunteers, Tennery, Hite, Johnson, Inman, Henry, and Perryman, joined Company E of the Fourth Regiment of Illinois Volunteers as privates. Hite was soon appointed commissary sergeant for Company E and in December, 1846, was named quartermaster sergeant for the regiment.

[2] Probably First Lieutenant William A. Thomas, who commanded a company of the Third Illinois Regiment, which was recruited and served with the Fourth Regiment. Together they comprised the Third Brigade of the Volunteer Division.

[3] No Captain Wiley appears in the *Historical Register and Dictionary of the United States Army* as an army officer; however, use of military titles on the frontier was quite common.

July 2.—We struck our tent under the old oak where we lay last night, and got on the way a little after sunrise, passed through Amity, which is nine miles west of Greenville. After we left Amity we travelled through some handsome prairie, of rich and undulating plains on which are a great many rich and beautiful farms. About nine miles west of Amity on the road is a singular place. It consists of a layer of stone about four feet square on top and two [feet] thick, placed two or three inches apart are these lines parallel cutting each other at right angles; this platform of stone extends under the banks of the bottom (which is nine or ten rods wide) to an unknown extent. These stones are a species of hard sand stone and must have been placed there by the hand of man. At twelve o'clock we passed Marine, to the left of the Alton road about a quarter of a mile. This evening we reached the great American bottom and travelled in it about six miles until we reached the rising ground where we camped in the woods by a little bank, one mile and a half from Alton.

July 3.—Drove into upper Alton; here for the first time we got a view of the camp. What emotions thrill the heart at the sight of a military camp to which one expected or wished to be attached; all the vain-glory of war will rush onto the mind; in an instant we take the turn, our minds are at home with sister, brother or tender parent; we half wish ourselves there. We soon found there was no difficulty in getting into Colonel Baker's regiment, to whom we had letters of introduction, for which we feel grateful to some of the distinguished citizens of Shelbyville.[4] Six of us joined

[4] The concern shown by Tennery in obtaining letters of recommendation appears not to have been without cause. Illinois was asked for four regiments; fourteen volunteered.

Colonel Edward Dickenson Baker was born in London in 1811 and went to Philadelphia with his parents in 1815. In 1825 the family

Company E [commanded by] Capt. Newcombe[5] from De Witt County; then we went down to lower Alton to see Capt. Freeman's[6] company of Shelby County. Here we found the Shelby boys in fine case. Johnson was taken dangerously sick here, we left him in care of Peter McNeil and Henry to take care of him until tomorrow.

July 4.—This morning we rose in our tents at the beat of the reveille for the first time, obtained leave of the captain this morning; went down to lower Alton, found Johnson better. Cary and Hinton left for home this morning with the team. Alton is situated on the river, it has a broken hilly site, and is abundantly supplied with limestone for building material. There are a goodly number of springs in this vicinity, one called the Spring Cave, about a quarter of a mile up a branch[7] from Alton, runs out of a cave, about seventy-five yards in the bank where the cave terminates, there is a water fall, which keeps up a constant noise. We received orders this evening to march down to ship for

moved to New Harmony, Indiana, and a year later to Belleville, Illinois. By the age of nineteen Baker had been admitted to the bar, and by twenty he had married a widow with two children. He served as a private in the Black Hawk War and then moved to Springfield, where he practiced law and engaged in politics with Lincoln, Douglas, and others. He served in the lower house of the state legislature from 1837 to 1840 and in the upper house from 1840 to 1844. He was elected to Congress in 1844, defeating Lincoln for the Whig nomination. Though a Whig, he supported Polk on the Oregon question. When the Mexican War began, he returned to Illinois and raised a regiment, the Fourth Illinois. In December, 1846, he returned to Washington and in uniform addressed the House to plead for supplies and equipment. He then resigned his seat, joined his regiment at Tampico, and won distinction at Cerro Gordo, where he commanded the brigade after General Shields was wounded (see note 32 below).

[5] Captain Daniel Newcomb.

[6] Captain James Freeman, who commanded a company of the Third Regiment.

[7] Tennery regularly used "branch" to mean a creek or small stream.

Jefferson barracks, so after packing the baggage, our mess, with the leave of the captain, went by Captain Freeman's camp to get Johnson, whom we found able to walk down to town. After bidding our acquaintance good-bye we joined our regiment in town; this was about dusk; here we stood on the bank until about twelve o'clock waiting for boats.

July 5.—Near one this morning the boats came to the wharf, we got aboard and sailed for the barracks, which we reached about six o'clock. The barracks are twelve miles below St. Louis, on the river bluff about fifty feet above the water. It is built of limestone and in the form of a hollow square containing about three acres with the end to the river open, the width is about one half of the length. The buildings in the west end are two-story, without the cellars, also the houses on the ends of the side rows next the river; the three enclosed sides have alleys or pass-ways in the center of them, the rooms for common soldiers are one story high without the cellar, which makes them two on the outside. There are porches on each side of the buildings, those on the outside having their floors about nine feet above ground which gives them a healthy appearance. The hospital is a large two story brick building about one hundred yards north of the guard house, which is about four yards north of the north crossway passage; off northeast of the guard-house is the market house, still further out is the residence and garden of Col. Davenport,[8] who is the present commander of the barracks. The river rubs the east side of his garden. The commissary house is down on the river bank east of the south line of the barracks; still down the river bank five or six rods from it are the stables; west of the stables are the pastures, about two hundred yards west of the south

[8] Colonel William Davenport, a veteran of the War of 1812 and the Seminole War. He was to retire in 1850.

line of the barracks is the store, out south of it is the post-office and three or four hundred yards west of the barracks is the church, besides there are other buildings scattered about too numerous to mention.

July 6.—Nothing today of importance, drill four hours a day.

July 7.—A great deal of complaining about rations in bread.

July 8.—Almost everyone complaining about diarrhea.

July 10.—Strong talk with some of deserting.

July 11.—This evening we witnessed the burial of a brother volunteer [Alex McGarvey]. He belonged to Co. I. His body was borne to the grave on a bier covered with the barracks flag, accompanied by the whole company, and band of the garrison. Two of his brothers stood by his grave. Who could stand by and not feel for those affectionate brothers, bereaved of one dear to them; oh how it will rend their hearts to let their families know of this sad event.

July 12.—This day is the Sabbath, no drill. We spent the time reading, picking blackberries, walking or sitting in the shade.

July 13.—Captain Page,[9] who had his jaw shot away in the battle of the fifth of May was buried here this evening. He died on his way to this place yesterday morning at three o'clock aboard the steamboat *Missouri.* The funeral was a grand but solemn scene. The regiment paraded and marched out in platoons, until the head of the column reached the road, then wheeled to the left and halted at the church. We, being not well, went on and stepped into the church, where the corpse lay, before the chaplain who was making some appropriate remarks to the congregation, and com-

[9] Captain John Page, who had been wounded on May 8 at the Battle of Palo Alto.

mending his wife and children to the friend of the widow, and father of the orphans. After prayer the coffin was carried and placed in the hearse. At this moment the sun was sinking behind the western horizon encircled by golden edged clouds, the wind blew gently from the north waving the colors toward the graveyard. The band of music accompanied the hearse to the grave playing a funeral air, followed by the regiment. When the music ceased, all halted, the pall-bearers approached the hearse, bore the body to its long home, three volleys blazed over the open grave, breaking the death like silence, and illuminating the approaching dusk. A few of us filled the grave and left him to sleep until—no more and the trumpet shall again call forth. Again the graveyard receives the body of another man as its lawful heir, he was a regular who died of insanity. For a few days past we have seen enough to impress on our minds the prediction "dust thou art, and unto dust shalt thou return."

July 15.—This morning two deserters fetched in; how bad they must feel after disgracing themselves. General Orders to join the army of General Taylor on the Rio Grande.

July 16.—General Crohern[10] commenced the inspection of regiment, and inspected two companies and they received payment; all in fine humor this evening.

July 17.—No inspection or pay today.

July 18.—Col. Churchill[11] commenced the inspection

[10] Colonel George Croghan, inspector general, U.S. Army, from 1825 until his death in 1849. Zachary Taylor mentioned him favorably for his conduct at Monterrey. He then returned to the United States to attend to his duties as inspector general.

[11] Colonel Sylvester Churchill, another inspector general, U.S. Army, from 1841 to 1861, succeeding General John E. Wool. He was in command of the second section in Wool's movement from San Antonio to Saltillo. He commanded a unit under Wool at Buena Vista, and was breveted brigadier general for his service there.

again; inspected, sworn in, paid off forty-two dollars[12] each; finished paying about midnight. Inman and I got in an omnibus this morning and rode up to St. Louis then walked out five miles west to his uncle's where we had a pleasant time. We went to the sulphur springs; this rises in a branch bottom about one hundred and fifty yards wide. The water tastes strong of sulphur. Here is a grog shop, tenpin alley and every thing necessary to dissipation; through there is a beautiful growth of small timber, here, making a pleasant shade, carpeted with bluegrass. Also we went to coal mines, they consist of a bed of coal, three or four feet thick and from one or two, to forty or fifty under ground, this difference is owing to the unevenness of the ground. Some places the miners work straight under the banks; others sink holes down to the coal, which they lift with windlasses worked by horsepower.

July 19.—Returned to St. Louis and stayed until evening, got in a hack, went back to the barracks.

July 21.—On guard for the first time.

July 22.—Inman has gone to St. Louis to get our uniforms.[13] Henry is at the hospital; Perryman on guard. While we have orders to prepare to go on board steamboats tomorrow. Accordingly we pack up our baggage and send it on.

July 23.—The regiment got aboard the steamboats *Sultan* and *Eclipse*: our Company got aboard the former with four other companies. Both the boats sailed to St. Louis, where

[12] Since a private's pay was seven dollars a month, this would appear to be six months' pay, though it was customary to pay army troops every two months (see entries for November 28, 1846, and February 20, 1847). Some of the funds may have represented uniform allowances. The men evidently purchased uniforms in St. Louis the following day (see entries for July 19 and 22).

[13] Equipping the thousands of volunteers continued to be a problem, as indicated by Baker's visit to Washington.

we stayed until seven o'clock P.M. then left for New Orleans.

July 24.—Got up this morning, the boat puffing its way down the river, passing some high bluffs on the right. This evening we pass the mouth of the Kaskaskia.[14]

July 25.—We pass the grand tower today. This celebrated tower is nothing more than a sugar-loaf shaped rock, that rises off the water close to the Missouri shore, and is a portion of the bluff, that has withstood the current of the river. It is covered with a small growth of timber. Above this a little, on the Illinois side are two rocks like the former but larger, they are called the devil's bake-oven; still above this is Fountain Bluff. This bluff and the one on the Missouri side must, to all appearance have been joined together at one time, forming one of the most stupendous cascades that ever fell down a precipice.

July 26.—Got to the mouth of the Ohio this morning, landed at Cairo, freighted on some lead.[15] Bid goodbye to Illinois.

July 27.—Landed at Memphis about twelve; here are the *Eclipse* and a boat load of Colonel Forman's[16] troops. Across the river is camped a regiment of Tennessee cavalry.[17]

[14] The Kaskaskia runs through Tennery's home town of Shelbyville and empties into the Mississippi about two hundred miles downstream.

[15] Lead was mined in Missouri across the river from Cairo, Illinois, as well as in Illinois itself, and bulk quantities were transported to be cast into musket balls.

[16] Colonel Ferris Foreman, commander of the Third Illinois Infantry, which served with the Fourth Regiment throughout the war.

[17] This regiment of Tennessee Cavalry was the subject of a book, *The Twelve Month Volunteer*, published in 1848 by George C. Farber, a member of that command. The Tennessee Cavalry marched overland across Arkansas and Texas, met the Third and Fourth Illinois on the Río Grande, and marched with them to Victoria and Tampico. Though Tennery does not mention the fact, Generals John A. Quitman, William O. Butler, and Gideon J. Pillow were in Memphis at the time, on their way to New Orleans and on to the Río Grande.

July 28.—Past Vicksburg last night and Natchez today; here the boys fetched me some fresh figs and peaches.

July 29.—Landed at the lower part of [New] Orleans about twelve o'clock. We quarter upstairs in a large warehouse. The *Eclipse* landed about ten this evening. I am nearly well of the ague, which I had to come on me just after we got to the lower Mississippi.

July 30.—The troops came off the *Eclipse* this morning. This evening companies A, B, C, E, and G got aboard this ship, the *Sea Lion.*

July 31.—The other companies, H excepted, are getting aboard of two other small vessels.[18] Evening all aboard fast to a towboat gliding down the river, pass the old battle ground, cheers from Col. Forman's troops who are quartered here. I had almost forgot to remark that Capt. McConkey received an accidental wound in the thigh. This was a ball from a pistol in the hands of H. C. McReynolds, his first lieutenant.[19]

General Robert Patterson, who commanded Tennery's column to Tampico, and General Butler were the two major generals of volunteers. There were six brigadier generals of volunteers: James Shields, Pillow, Quitman, Thomas Marshall, Thomas L. Hamer, and Joseph Lane. Among the regulars, Generals Taylor and Winfield Scott were the only major generals, and Wool, David E. Twiggs, and Stephen Watts Kearney were the only brigadiers. Franklin Pierce and George Cadwalader were appointed later, in 1847.

[18] Generals Butler, Quitman, Pillow, Wool, Shields, and Marshall sailed on the *New York* with two companies of the Illinois Infantry.

[19] Captain John S. McConkey, who commanded Company H of the Fourth Illinois Infantry. H. C. McReynolds remains a mystery. He does not appear on the company roster as McConkey's executive; in fact, he does not appear on any roster in the Fourth Regiment or elsewhere, and no name resembling his appears in the *Historical Register*. One explanation may be that the embarrassment and disgrace he suffered because of his ineptitude as a soldier was so great that he went home forthwith and was never entered on the roster.

August 1.—We came out by the southwest pass. The gulf spreads away to the south with ships lying here and there at anchor, or moving out or in lashed to tow boats. We busy ourselves by looking out on the gulf or climbing among the rigging of the vessel. The mouth of the pass embanked on each side by mold or loam of river mud extends a long way into the gulf. Here are a great many porpoises plunging about in the fresh water. After towing us out about twenty miles farther in the gulf, the boat left us. Here the salt water begins to mix with the river water, making blue places in it. Out on the west of the pass is a lighthouse.

August 2.—Nothing but blue water and sky in view, except a few sails in sight, and an occasional shark playing around the ship; the longest we saw was nine or ten feet.

August 3.—Almost no wind. The boys amuse themselves watching the fish, especially a little kind that rises out of the water and sails along in the air three or four rods. These flying fish are about four inches long and rise in flocks; they fly by means of two long fins on the back.

August 4.—Clear this morning with scattering clouds. This evening there is appearance of a storm, about three o'clock there was a water-spout in the west. This singular phenomenon appeared like a column of water to reach to the clouds. It appeared about the thickness of a large ship mast, this faded away gradually.

August 5.—Squalls of wind with rain.

August 6.—We hove in sight of sandbanks west of us and sailed along them all day. The curiosity excited by the deep has subsided, and we long to be on shore where seasickness will cease. About sundown the ship tacked off to east to clear the bar.

August 7.—Last night a little squall of wind and rain struck the ship which made those sleeping on deck tumble down the hatchway at a fearful rate one over another, some crawling off on all fours. One poor fellow rolled off the cabin and got badly hurt. The fright over, as an opposite feeling is sure to follow, in excitement we gave away to immoderate laughter. We are still sailing along the reef with a headwind.

August 8.—How amusing it is to one who can keep calm in an excited multitude, when all wish to be heard and none know the cause; except all wished to be on shore. Still sailing along the bar.

August 9.—Anchored this morning in sight of shore, all are in high spirits, the Col. has gone on shore to get boats. Twelve o'clock, all is hurry and bustle and moving of baggage. We got on shore at dusk off the steamship, which ferried us to shore.[20] How the feelings change when one first steps on shore from his first voyage at sea. He treads the earth with a light heart, and feels he has escaped a hundred dangers. The earth appears more lovely, the air more pure and the stars, planets and moon appear more bright. In fact when the mind is satisfied all nature is lovely. After considering our present situation, the mind turns to home. We see our friends in the family group, sitting by the fireside, our place is vacant, a sister's or a brother's half broken sigh bespeaks their feelings. How gladly we would resign the campaign to be there, yes, in the family circle where after the toils of the day were over and the stars begin to appear one by one, we sat on father's knee with a twin sized brother and learned their names; or ranged in the class in the morning to hear a chapter from the word of God; or after a hard day's schooling witnessed the smiles of a pious mother as she turned her eyes to father and said my boys are learning to

[20] They landed at Brazos Island on August 12 and waded across Boca Chica to the mainland.

read the Bible. But why should we treasure up these things in the minds. They are gone to return no more.

August 10.—After a night's rest, on shore we got our baggage divided, tents up and examined the shore, picked up shells and waded out, gathered oysters, bathed in the gulf, visited friends; dress parade, a few words of advice from the Colonel.

August 11.—We occupied our leisure time by bathing, exploring the coast in search of shells or wading. This evening this company received orders to go up the Rio Grande tomorrow, to clear off an encampment for their regiment.

August 12.—A hard rain last night. All is hurry in our company this morning. As soon as breakfast was over we packed our clothing in the knapsacks for the first time, and left tents and provisions in care of Sergeant Vinson.[21] All that were able took up the line of march with packs on back for the river, travelled down the coast about two miles where we crossed a bay or inlet by wading close to the breakers; then marched west about eight miles through low sandy plains, sometime mud and water interspersed with ridges four or five feet high covered with a small growth of brush called chaparral eight or ten feet high. Here we came to the river; this stream is full to the top of the channel in places, and the boats on the water look at a distance like as if they were on the open prairie. We travelled up the river some distance, turned to the right to a chaparral ridge where we began to clear off the camp ground; we have to use water which has to be carried a quarter of a mile.

August 13.—Here[22] are camped seven or eight thousand troops from different states; though everyone seems to have connections in each state, and it is amusing to see friends

[21] Sergeant John Vinson, one of the four sergeants in Company E.
[22] Camp Belknap.

meet. Let those who are vain or ignorant enough, to talk of a disunion in the United States, be silent forever, when they consider the ties of kindred and the feelings existing from Maine to the Rio Grande, and from Florida to Oregon. The regiment came out today. No baggage arrived yet.

August 14.—We slept last night in the open air without tents. The baggage is at the mouth of the river. Three teams came up this evening with some provisions and cooking utensils. There are prickly pears growing in abundance about this place, also cayenne peppers. It would be proper to remark all the bushes are thorny; there are crabs, lizards, spiders, ants and frogs in abundance here.

August 15.—Nothing today of importance. The baggage came up on a steamboat; the commissary stores are still behind. Everyone appears cheerful and happy, and there is many a merry laugh or cheerful song wafted on the pleasant breeze.

August 16.—I awoke this morning with pains in the bowels, but after stirring a little got better. Just after dinner I was taken with vomiting and cramps in the bowels which made me very sick, but I had all the attention required. Ye everlasting powers forbid that I should be so ungrateful to ever forget the kind care and attention bestowed upon me by messmates. No commissary stores have come yet.

August 17.—We are all well today, nothing of importance occurred today.

August 18.—The Edgar County boys [Company H] came up today, they have been behind ever since we left Orleans. The commissary stores came up today.

August 19.—We went out today and gathered a quantity of cayenne peppers, which grew spontaneous in the chaparral groves on a vine that runs up of a thorny bush and weeds in abundance.

August 20.—Nothing of importance.

August 21.—There has been no rain since we came to this place, but there have generally been cool breezes blowing off the gulf, and flying clouds.

August 22.—The mind of man is always on the march, first forward then about face counter-march, wheeling and maneuvering at will like its divine author, it never sleeps, no wonder then we are lying here without anything to amuse us, we have a great deal of camp news.

August 23.—This day is Sunday, and no doubt there is many a mind turned to home; in their imaginations they see friends in the church bending before a throne of grace, invoking the eternal for prosperity of the nation and our return in safety.

August 24.—We have had a shower of rain this morning; the ground is wet which makes it hard drilling. About nine o'clock a prairie wolf was started up the river and came down past the Indiana troops, and Col. Forman's regiment where it received some kicks and blows, not being used to such treatment he stopped to look at the crowd a few rods in front but seeing some horses and all rushing bawling at him, he was taken with a leaving; three or four horsemen followed him two or three miles but gave up the chase.

August 25.—Jerry McPherson[23] of this company died last night. He was a fine young man, who left his home in as fine spirits as any one. But alas we have to leave him beneath the sandy turf of the chaparral grove. By him lie some of the Kentucky troops. There are interred in this vicinity a great

[23] Disease and illness took the lives of about one in ten of all volunteers in the Mexican War. Private Jesse L. McPherson is recorded as having died at Camp Patterson on August 25, 1846; Corporal L. Martin Bennet, of Company C, on August 31; and Private Charles W. Dillon, also of Company C, on September 1 (see entries for August 30 and 31).

many men from the states, and a funeral or two takes place every day. We should expect deaths to take place in an army like this, almost constantly, and be prepared for the worst at a moment's warning.

August 26.—Past a review of five o'clock P.M. The commissary bought and butchered three beeves, this was an interesting sight to many of us as the Mexicans who had been hired by the drover lassoed them; this is done by a rope that a horseman holds in a large coil, with one end fast to the pommel of the saddle and the other with a noose, hurled round and thrown over the head or horns, then he dashes spurs to his horse and guides him in another direction until he jerks down the beef or stops his horse if he does not succeed the first time he wraps the rope about its legs and tries to again until he throws and holds it until the butcher cuts its throat.

August 27.—We had a hard rain today about twelve o'clock and it remained cloudy all evening.

August 28.—This has been a cloudy day. Theophilus Johnson has the mumps; they are going through the regiment at this time and are tolerable bad this damp hot weather.

August 29.—Inman lost his purse containing twenty-five dollars in gold and five cents in silver, with some papers. It is thought that it was taken by some low bred pickpockets while he was in a crowd looking at some men who were performing some theatrical trick in Company A, but he appears not to care much and no doubt feels better by ten degrees, [his] self-respect real content, better than the conscience of the condemned down-cast imp who stole it.

August 30.—We had a hard rain last night and this morning; the ground is very wet, but the sky faired off about seven or eight o'clock. We cut and piled about three acres of brush adjoining our camp on the north today. There was another brother soldier buried, he belonged to Co. C. He lies beneath this chaparral grove; with prickly pears growing his grave above.

August 31.—Co. C lost another man to-day at four o'clock, the funeral was at Nine P.M. Just as the procession arrived at the grave, our attention was drawn by the noise of a riot in the Georgian troops; as the notice of the battle continued to rage, as soon as the funeral volleys were fired, Colonel Baker took men and went down to the river, but left orders for companies A and G to form and come on. When he got there, he found the riot was in the upper part of the boat. The lieutenant-colonel invited him to come on and help him put a stop to it. Accordingly he went on up accompanied by Capt. Hirt[24] and some others who were drawn by the noise.

As soon as he got up he began to call on them to cease fighting. No sooner was his manly voice heard to rise above the noise of the melee than one of the captains of the fighting parties rushed at him with drawn sword in his hand which put Baker under the necessity of warding off the blow with his scabbard and drawing his sword at the same time; but he defended himself and cut his antagonist across the mouth and would no doubt have felled him to the floor, had not one of his men rushed up and shot the Colonel in the neck. Captain Hirt it is said played a musket which he happened to have in his hand like a giant; in the meantime, Lieutenant Oglesby[25] who was commanding the funeral squad succeeded in getting his men on the boiler deck and in

[24] Captain John C. Hurt, commander of Company I of the Fourth Illinois Infantry. For a contemporary account of the riot, see the Appendix at the end of this book.

[25] First Lieutenant Richard J. Oglesby, the second officer in Company C, Fourth Illinois Infantry.

forming them where they were attacked almost instantly by the fighting parties, but stood to it like veterans, not to be daunted by overpowering numbers. Some of the Georgians succeeded in getting behind Oglesby's men and were bayonetting those who attempted to come up. At this moment Captains Jones[26] and Roberts[27] attempted to lead up their men, but Captain Roberts being struck on the shoulder with a bayonet while on the stair, one man cried out "I have a ball in my gun. Shall I use it?" "Yes" was the reply. He stepped two paces out of ranks, raised his gun to his face and blazed away. Down fell the man who was defending the stairs and his companions disappeared. At this, some one stepped forward and said "If you please do not bring the Illinois troops on here and kill all the men for the fuss is about stopped now." Thus with the firmness and hard fighting of the twenty or at most thirty men of Col. Baker's [he] saved his life by jumping overboard on the land side; one Miles Brainard grabbed his sword [as] soon as he was shot and defended him until he made the leap, then followed him; the rest were ordered down.

So the grit and courage of thirty men stopped a riot, where two companies were engaged. By the time it was over three regiments were on the ground in front of the boat with ball and cartridge in their guns. They placed guards around the boat and kept out part of one company that the funeral detail found preparing to use their guns and arrested when they first got there and placed under guard. There were two companies on the boat that were on the bow or that had no hand in the row from first to last. And Colonel

[26] Captain Edward Jones, commander of Company G, Fourth Illinois Infantry.

[27] Captain Horatio E. Roberts, commander of Company A, Fourth Illinois Infantry.

Baker has found the proverb true: "he who meddleth with strife is like one that taketh a dog by the ears." In doing what he thought to be his duty he was badly wounded and got eleven more wounded, one mortally; he was shot through the bowels by a ball and two shot. Commissary [Joel Seth] Post was shot at the same time in the breast, but it is only a slight flesh wound; the men behaved well.

September 1.—We do not know how many of the Georgians were slain last night, but one was found this morning on board; he was the man who was shot at the head of the stairs. It is thought that the slain were thrown overboard. Captain Newcomb went through the boat just after the fray and saw several dead on the floor, and could hear the blood scrush under the carpet from one boat's [end] to the other; and a man belonging to one of the companies on the deck says he was present at roll call and at least twenty-five were slain or missing. They were marched out without arms this morning and taken up to Colonel Moses Marcy[28] where they were unarmed and four were ordered to be put in irons and the officers of one company under arrest and [he] put them on the *Corvette* again and sent them up the river. The Lieutenant-Colonel's name is Real.[29] The man who was mortally wounded died and was buried this evening. Captain McConkey came up this evening; he is nearly well.

28 Not identified. Colonel Henry R. Jackson commanded the Georgia Regiment. The secretary of war was William L. Marcy, a descendant of Moses Marcy, the founder of Sturbridge, Massachusetts. It is possible that Moses Marcy was a member of the secretary's family sent to the front to represent him and assigned the rank of colonel for the purpose. No Moses Marcy is listed as having served as an officer in the United States Army.

29 Lieutenant Colonel Thomas Y. Redd, second-in-command of the Georgia Regiment. Regiments normally had one colonel, one lieutenant colonel, and one major.

September 2.—Nothing occurred of importance.

September 3.—We were inspected today.

September 4.—A great deal of talk of getting discharged and sent home.

September 5.—Nothing today of importance but camp news and of all places in America, camp is the greatest for news. Every man being accustomed to form and spend his opinion on all subjects, and still takes the liberty to tell all he hears and sometimes what he thinks for truth.

September 6.—One Mr. Smith [Private Himelion Smith] died last night of Co. H. He is the first of that company lost. Colonel Baker has gone up the river, with several other officers of this regiment. Just after dusk a boat came down the river with some Texas rangers aboard, and landed on the opposite side.

September 7.—We had a hard shower of rain last night, and this is a cloudy, wet morning. There was a rather novel circumstance occurred this morning. A flock of quail settled in the encampment and most of them were caught by the soldiers: they are the same species as live in Illinois. This evening we walked out north of the encampment to the point of this ridge, and it is truly a place for a post; we can hear the loud but distant roar of the gulf, the howl of the solitary prairie wolf, the croaking of frogs of various kinds and the chirping of hundreds of insects, mingled with splashing water in the overgrown bottom by toads, crabs and waterfowl; while to the south is the long line of encampments illuminated by a thousand candles, while the hum and noise roar like the roar of the distant gulf, and the retiring clouds still give out their faint flashes of light; add to this the groan of a distant steamer, the silver light of the rising moon, the bright sheets of water with the almost viewless groves beyond them, with the calm fresh air and the blue heavens bespangled with millions of gems of light. Contemplating scenes like this the mind is lost in reverie and when consciousness returns we find our hides chilled and our locks wet with the dews of the night, which makes us return to the tent and wrap ourselves in the arms of restorative sleep.

September 8.—[Private] Isaac Richards [Company E] died last night at two o'clock. He was an excellent young man about five feet four inches with a heavy well set frame, dark hazel eyes shaded with heavy brows and thin black mustache and thin curly whiskers on the back of cheeks, with quick voice and ready wit, with a smiling countenance and a kind of little trick which kept the company in mirth and gave him the nickname of "Short" and "Goody." Though universally beloved by all who knew him and deplored by the company, we have to consign him to the grave to be forgotten by all his friends but those dear to him by the law of nature.

September 9.—Nothing today of note, but company B has lost a young man [Private Andrew J. Hodge] who it is said was the favorite child of his father. Alas, what tears of contrition will flow for those who die in the army without a mother, wife or sister to smooth the pillow or close their eyes in death and weep over their bier; but their friends when they get the sad tidings should sustain the loss with a Christian fortitude knowing that they died in the service of their country surrounded by their fellow soldiers who did all in their power for them.

September 10.—Again I have to record the death of two more soldiers—one of this company, Calvin Payne[30] who died at daybreak this morning; he was a good man; the other

[30] Private Calvin Payne is recorded as having died at Camp Patterson on September 10, 1846.

was [Private Alonzo A. Yan] of Co. K. They were buried within a few minutes of each other, we have to lay the dead in the vault without coffin or box, for the boards or plank cannot be found in this place.

September 11.—Three companies of this regiment went up the river today. We will all go up to within a few miles of Matamoros as fast as we can get conveyance.

September 12.—Three more companies started up the river this evening in which ours is included, and commissary Hite and I are all that are left of the company.

September 13.—This morning the Sabbath sun rose upon the encampment something like it used to on our peaceful homes for us; there are but four companies of the regiment here, all is comparatively still and but few laughs or loud words are heard to rise on the encampment. Autumn here resembles the same season in Illinois. This has been a clear day, with faint sunshine, cool air stirring and an occasional floating cloud. Co. K started up this evening on board the *Warren*.

September 14.—Ungrateful is he who does not feel lonely and dejected when he sees a village or neighborhood deserted where he has resided for a length of time; such are our feelings at present, for we have been here a month and have grown familiar with the place, and attached to our shade trees, but as fast as the men leave the Indiana men come and cut them down. Co. H left this afternoon, and before all of their tents were moved off the ground the shade was prostrated. The day corresponds with our feelings. Since twelve o'clock the southern half of the horizon has been covered with a black cloud from which we can hear muttering thunder.

September 15.—We are anxiously waiting for a boat to take us up the river, but are surprised this evening by the

Big Hatchy, which we expected to go up on, stopping here without orders to take any of us, consequently we have to report to the quartermaster at Brazos that he may send a boat with orders to take us which will detain us a day or two longer.

September 16.—Today Mr. Hite rode up the river to see the country, and was much pleased with the trip though he found nothing but sandy ridges and wet overgrown prairie inhabited by wolves, armadilloes and a large species of hare, besides cranes and countless numbers of the heron kind; also a species of eagle like the bald eagle but not so large.

September 17.—I had a ride this morning and evening; went out and gathered crabs, we caught them in water where it was shoe-mouth deep, and boiled them in the messpan and ate them for supper. The steamboat *Exchange* landed here this evening to take us up tomorrow.

September 18.—This morning we moved the baggage to the river and sent the teams and horses over to go up by land; got aboard and left at twelve o'clock, for Camp Patterson. We soon passed Beretee [Burrita], which is three miles above the old camp ground, on the Mexican side of the river. This town is situated on a ridge close to the river and consists of a dozen or two miserable huts or houses made of sticks placed in the ground picket fashion and daubed with mud, and covered with coarse grass or palmetto. The ridges have asses and a few horned cattle grazing on them; some miles above, we came to the tilled land where we saw a good many patches of corn, which is ripe and dry, fenced by sticks stuck in the ground or brush piled along in rows. We landed to wood this evening at a farm where there is corn growing. It is in silk and tassle at present. The wood is chaparral cut and corded at two dollars a cord by the Mexicans; they have plenty of cattle, but the houses are quite indifferent.

Major Thomas L. Harris, third-ranking officer of the Fourth Illinois Infantry (Tennery's regiment), after Colonel Edward D. Baker and Lieutenant Colonel John Moore. This portrait was made in the 1850's when Harris was a member of the United States House of Representatives.

ILLINOIS STATE ARCHIVES

Colonel Edward D. Baker, commander of the Fourth Illinois Infantry (Tennery's regiment). He was a member of Congress at the time of the outbreak of the Mexican War, and he later served in the United States Senate. He was killed early in the Civil War.

ILLINOIS STATE ARCHIVES

Brigadier General James Shields, Colonel Baker's immediate superior. He was a friend of Lincoln, served in the United States House of Representatives, and later successively represented three different states in the United States Senate. He is shown here as a senator in about 1860.

NATIONAL ARCHIVES

Zachary Taylor, who in 1849 went from victories in Mexico to the White House, where he died the following year.

NATIONAL ARCHIVES

Brigadier General John Ellis Wool, one of the five Regular Army generals in the Mexican War. He is shown here at the time of his promotion to major general in 1861.

NATIONAL ARCHIVES

Brevet Major General David E. Twiggs, one of the five Regular Army generals in the Mexican War, shown here with the sword presented to him by Congress in 1854 for his service in that war. He resigned to join the Confederate Army in 1861.

NATIONAL ARCHIVES

Major General Winfield Scott in dress uniform during the Civil War. He was then over eighty years old, and had been a general for fifty years. He was responsible for the defeat of Mexico.

NATIONAL ARCHIVES

Gideon Johnson Pillow, President Polk's law partner and the first brigadier general of volunteers to be promoted to major general. He is shown here after he resumed his law practice. He served in the Confederate Army in the Civil War.

NATIONAL ARCHIVES

Colonel William Selby Harney, General Scott's cavalry chief in the Mexican War, in which he served with distinction. He is shown here as a brigadier general at the beginning of the Civil War.

NATIONAL ARCHIVES

John Anthony Quitman, shown here as a member of Congress in the 1850's, a brigadier general of volunteers in the Mexican War.

NATIONAL ARCHIVES

September 19.—We awoke on board this morning at the camp, got ashore and found that three men had died since the regiment came here [Privates William Beason and Joseph Donavan of Company I and Temple Souther of Company C]. This is a level place covered with chaparral and small brush with a good many farms, or small patches of cleared and inclosed land where the inhabitants live. They are a mixed race of people of Spanish, Indian and Negro; their language is adulterated Spanish. They appear to know but little about agriculture or the peaceful arts, and live chiefly by their herds of cattle and horses; they make bread by boiling corn soft and rolling it between a cast roller and board until they form paste or dough fit for the oven.

September 20.—Sunday, clear and pleasant, four companies ordered to Camargo, they got aboard of the *Colonel Cross*[31] and left a little after dark. Another funeral today. General Shields[32] left for Wool's[33] division this evening.

September 21.—Rainy and wet. This encampment being in a level place of loam bottom it is very muddy and disagreeable getting about. James Perryman is sick this evening, which leaves but three of us to do anything as Henry and Inman have been unwell for several days.

September 22.—Autumnal equinox, a fair day, we have

[31] Named for Colonel Trueman Cross, U.S. Army quartermaster, who was killed April 21, 1846, by Mexican bandits.

[32] General James Shields, commander of the Third Brigade of Illinois Volunteers, one of the six brigadiers appointed by Polk on July 1, 1846. Like Colonel Baker, he was an attorney, served in the Black Hawk War, and resigned from Congress to serve in the Mexican War. Wounded at Cerro Gordo, he was breveted major general (see note 4 above).

[33] General John E. Wool, who entered the army as a captain in 1812 and was breveted lieutenant colonel in 1814 for gallant conduct at Plattsburg. He was breveted brigadier general in 1826 and by 1841 was a brigadier general. He was promoted to major general in 1847 for gallant and meritorious conduct at Buena Vista.

been out walking and are well pleased with the country, the air being perfumed with flowers, the morning glory, lily, and a large weed with red blossoms like the hollyhock grow spontaneously in abundance here. And various others such as the fall flowers and vines, weeds and grasses not known in Illinois. The castor bean grows beautifully along the river banks, without cultivation.

September 23.—The ground is drying off which makes it pleasant getting about again; it is rather warm in the daytime and cool at nights.

September 24.—We packed up this evening and all that were able started for Matamoros and left the sick to come up on a boat with the tents and baggage. Not being accustomed to it the marching was very fatiguing to us. The road runs up the river through a level country, thickly settled. Crossing several swamps and one through which we waded in water above the knees, at last we reached town after marching nine or ten miles; our shoulders are chafed, knees weak and tongues most parched with thirst. Quartered in large brick buildings.

September 25.—We awoke this morning after a night's sleep in the famed and long wished for city, the city Matamoros. This is a well laid out town, with the streets running parallel cutting each other at right angles. But the squares are not well improved, a great many of them being used as gardens or orchards fenced by posts or sticks set in the ground wrapped or woven in with brush. The buildings in the main part of town are built of brick, one or two story high, the orchards consist of figs, peaches, oranges and so forth. The common or poorer houses are built of unburned brick, poles set in the ground and daubed with mud and reeds tied together and set on end. From the second class houses to the lowest class, all are covered with weeds, palmetto and grass, cane and so forth. The sidewalks are paved with brick, but the main parts of the streets are muddy with puddle holes every here and there. The roofs of the good buildings are generally flat after the eastern or Asiatic fashion. The arts are in a low state; oxen are worked by a yoke fastened on the head, tied behind the horns. The most common way of hauling about the farm is on carts with wooden wheels, the most of the wood and hay consumed in this place is packed in on asses, mules or horses and it is not uncommon to see a little old jack or mule driven through the streets with nearly a cord of wood lashed on its back or a hundred [weight] or so of hay.

September 26.—The *Big Hatchee* came up last night bringing up the commissary stores and the sick with the two companies of the third regiment which were left there. So we left town and marched out north west of it and camped about four hundred yards from the river on a bayou. This is a beautiful green carpeted with bluegrass. Down below about five hundred yards is Fort Parados [Paredes]. It is built in a circular form containing about an acre; the wall is dirt or clay thrown up eight or nine feet high, mounted with cannon, and a deep ditch twelve or fourteen feet deep around the outside; it is occupied by soldiers at present. South of the encampment are many lakes or ponds about Matamoros. This division of the army is ordered to stay here; accordingly we expect the men at Camargo will return to this place.

September 27.—A beautiful cool Sunday morning, about fifteen of us went up to town with Lieutenant Howard[34] to the Catholic church; this is built of brick and would be a splendid edifice were it finished. When I entered this place

[34] Second Lieutenant Benjamin Howard, Company E, Fourth Illinois Infantry, one of two second lieutenants in Tennery's company.

of public worship the priest was standing up preaching in the pulpit; his grey hairs, strong persuasive voice, and venerable appearance with the stillness of the place struck us with reverential awe and devotion, the preaching over the priest kneeling to the images and the lamps burning, the ministering garments appeared absurd to us but we could not censure a form because it did not concur with our preconceived opinions of religion. The shops are all open and business appears to be going on the same as any other day of the week. There was a man buried this evening of company A. He died in camp this morning.

September 28.—These are beautiful autumn, Indian-summer like days, cool nights but no frost. This morning a hare was scared up somewhere about the encampment. It ran through here once or twice to the great diversion and amusement of the men. It was larger than any I ever saw in Illinois.

September 29.—A steamboat came down from Camargo today and reported Taylor had taken Monter[r]ey on the twenty fourth after a three days' siege. That the Mexican commander capitulated on condition he should march his troops away with all of their small arms and the twenty-one rounds of cartridge, also that the armistice should continue twenty-eight days.

September 30.—I was at the hospital today. It presents quite a sorrowful aspect; there are some five or six different places where they are kept, these though large and spacious are crowded with sick from all parts of the Union. There are not beds or mattresses enough for the sick; consequently a great many have to lay on the brick floor, without anything but a blanket underneath them. The care taken of them is according to the nurses' disposition.

October 1.—We were paraded at nine o'clock this evening, marched out, formed a regiment, and [were] told that the citizens apprehended an attack from some Mexicans who, it was reported, had been seen in the vicinity by the rangers.

October 2.—Various tales in camp, the most prevalent is that Carlos[35] is not far from this place, with a body of cavalry; two companies went to town to help guard tonight.

October 3.—Official orders are received at this place and Forts Parados and Brown[36] to fire twenty-six rounds of cannon each in honor of the United States, on account of the surrender of Monterey.

October 4.—Sunday. We attended the Catholic church, marched up to town, and climbed up ladders to the top of the house in which Col. Clark[37] is stationed, and lay all night. The roof is flat and sideling made by sheeting over the upper joints and covering the whole with brick.

October 5.—Awoke this morning from our sleep between brick and blanket. This is the top of the house which is said to have been the headquarters of the Mexicans when they were here. It is on the west side of the square in front of the Catholic church. Adjoining are large squares enclosed by brick walls twelve or fourteen feet high. In these are oranges, figs and so forth.

[35] Probably General Antonio Canales, commander of Mexican irregulars at Matamoros.

[36] Fort Brown (today Brownsville, Texas), across the Río Grande from Matamoros. It was named for Major Jacob Brown, who built the fort on the orders of General Taylor. Brown entered the army as a private in the War of 1812 and died at Fort Brown on May 9, 1846, of wounds received on May 6 in defense of it. Taylor captured Matamoros on May 18, after having defeated the Mexican army at Resaca de la Palma on May 9.

[37] Colonel Charles Clark, commander of the Second Mississippi Infantry.

October 6.—Orders today to march to Camargo tomorrow.

October 7.—The wagons came to this place last night in two days from the mouth. We expect to go up [with them] in a few days.

October 8.—Orders this evening to be ready to march in the morning.

October 9.—At eight o'clock the wagons commenced loading our baggage for Camargo. We started at twelve, marched to town, dismissed ten minutes, then paraded, divided into three divisions each to accompany a train of wagons; marched about four miles south, camped in a swampy place for the sake of water.

October 10.—Up before day-break ready to march by sunup; took the road in a westerly direction behind one hundred and twenty-five wagons drawn by five mules making a troop about one mile long; about twelve we halted at a pond, and prepared and ate dinner. Again we took up the line of march through a swamp one mile long and half leg deep. Then on the hard road we came to a prairie. This is a beautiful level plain with large herds of cattle and horses grazing on it. Here the mules became frightened and ran away, two wagons ran out one or two miles, nobody hurt or wagons broken. Here three soldiers shot at a flock of wild geese and killed one. Halted after marching eighteen miles. Early this day someone killed a rattle snake six feet long, four inches in diameter, thirteen rattles and a button and left it in the road.

October 11.—We got an early start, travelled on a level road, passing through some beautiful prairies and chaparral alternately. Early in the day we saw a large grey forest wolf. Just afterwards a great many horses pestered the teamsters very much, running and trying to break through the train.

After travelling twenty miles we camped where a Spaniard lived. Here we had to use water out of a well: a Mexican drew it with a rope tied to the pommel of his saddle running on a swivel over the well attached to a large leather bucket. Thus by walking the horse backward and forward he drew the water.

October 13.—Last night a yellow boy in the service of the suttler in the train was stabbed in the back by a Mexican. We started a little after sunup and travelled about a mile in a straight wide cut road. As soon as we left this we struck a ridge: up to this place we have not seen any rising ground since we left Matamoros. About eleven we passed over a bed of limestone two rods wide; this is the first native stone we have seen since we landed on this side the gulf. We camped early this evening at a pond made by an embankment, made in a half circle to dam up a wet weather run; here the Mexicans live more scattering than usual.

October 14.—Again we stopped early at some Mexican farms. Here the boys got some watermelons and roasting ears at a bit[38] a dozen, a pond water to use but better than common; the country has been undulating today; there is considerable of a hill off to the right of us. The Mexicans have an Indian slave here. He is a stout good looking fellow, a prisoner of war I suppose.

October 15.—This morning we travelled through the chaparral about two hours. Captain Hirt shot a small species of eagle. It resembled the bald eagle a little, but with a tail more like a falcon. It is about three feet wide from one point of the wing to the other. They are very plenty in this country. We have come to a stony hilly country. We camped at

[38] In the eighteenth century, Americans cut silver pesos into eight pie-shaped "bits" (pieces of eight). Since a peso was worth 8 reales, each bit was worth 1 real, or 12½ cents.

an American farm and got some soft corn again; we have stinking pond water to use such as the Mexicans make use of all the time.

October 16.—Again on the road early, travelling through hilly country, crossed a dry run or two and some bottom places in which the water has dried away and left the ground white with salt, we soon got in sight of Camargo. We can see nothing to distinguish it but the steeple of a church; at length we have passed through town. It is an indifferent looking place and stands on the east side of the San Juan; we camped with our troops.

October 17.—This encampment is a dusty place close to the river. The wind blowing makes it very uncomfortable. Mr. Hite found some of his acquaintances, from his native place, in the Ohio regiment. In fact their Colonel is one of his old playmates.

October 18.—Camargo is on the east side of the San Juan river, three miles above its junction with the Rio Grande; in the centre it has some good houses but the larger portion are almost all miserable hovels, built of unburned brick or posts set in the ground and plastered with mud without floors. Such is the city of Camargo in the midst of a fertile country with two crops of corn growing in one season, and cotton of the finest quality; yams and sweet potatoes almost without cultivation and melons, pumpkins, etc., in abundance, besides peaches, figs, oranges, lemons and quinces, and with an everlasting stock range lasting all summer and winter.

October 20.—A cold cloudy morning, the third and fourth regiments are camped together, consequently we put out our guards together.

October 21.—The Mexicans in this vicinity have large

flocks of goats the flesh of which they eat. They are mostly large white goats. Still cloudy and cool.

October 22.—Johnson is taking the measles. Captain Newcombe came up today, also the Commissary Post and several of this regiment who were left at Matamoros.

October 23.—Dry and dusty with light dews at night. The corn in this vicinity is in roasting ear.

October 24.—A burying today, one [Pvt. Willis T. Nance] of Co. F.[39] The king of terrors still reigns without a rival save the blood of Jesus.

October 25.—Inspection of arms: no drill today. A strong south wind which makes the sand and dust very disagreeable; the more so as Inman and Johnson both have the measles.

October 26.—Still a high wind and dust, uncomfortable in the extreme.

October 27.—Johnson was very sick last night, his case is considered a doubtful one by the physician. Warm sunny day.

October 28.—As we have to be up all times of these nights we can hear the yelping of hundreds of prairie wolves in every direction, even in the very suburbs of the town, wolves, dogs and the crowing of cocks all forming a mingled noise not uncommon in the western villages of America.

October 29.—Near two o'clock this morning the second tent to the right of where Johnson is sick took fire from a candle and burnt out the end before the inmates awoke. Fortunately there was no air stirring. A cloudy morning.

October 30.—Cloudy and cool of a morning but clear windy and dusty through the great part of the day.

[39] Private Willis T. Nance, one of eight men of Company F who died in October, 1846.

October 31.—Inspection by a U.S. officer[40] today, this forenoon had been cloudy but clear in the afternoon. No indications of frost yet. The herbs and vines continue to bloom as though it were June or July, though they are mostly of the yellow and white species which would denote the later part of the season in our latitude.

November 1.—Sunday morning, cloudy and cool and a misting rain, the clouds vanish about ten o'clock leaving it a warm sunny day. This evening Captain Jones, Roberts and Oglesby came back from Monterey. This is a light moon. Tonight it is pleasant and the troops appear gay notwithstanding that from one to five are buried a day from the two regiments.

November 2.—Cool misty morning and a hot sunny day. At six P.M., William Wallace[41] of this company died. He was a noble young man loved and reverenced by all. This evening one of the most ridiculous circumstances occurred that I ever saw; two young men of Co. B fell out and walked out to the graveyard to settle their dispute in the old vulgar fashion of fist and skull. Almost immediately over they departed comrades. They were arrested before either of them were hurt badly.

November 3.—Buried Wallace this morning. Feeling unwell I walked out for exercise and recreation. The town cemetery attracted my attention; it is directly east of the church three or four hundred yards from the town, containing one fourth of an acre enclosed by a brick wall six feet high with an arch over the gate on top of which is a cross.

[40] Tennery probably means an officer of the Regular Army.

[41] In the company roster William Wallace is recorded as having died on November 3, Ambrose Kinney on November 11, and David Beebe on November 14, all at Camargo (see entries for November 11 and 14).

The inside of this place is a disgusting place to look upon. In the center is a stile of brick with a cross on top with several skulls piled about the foot of it; besides various small crosses standing or leaning over the graves. All over this yard or depot for the dead, are human bones. In one corner are the ashes of someone of distinction enclosed in brick.

November 4.—We had a hard shower of rain this morning though the dry sandy ground dried it up almost immediately. This is a cool pleasant moonlight night.

November 5.—These cool mornings make the fog rise off the river, which obscured the sun until eight or nine o'clock this A.M.

November 6.—Nothing of importance. The river glides along as smooth as ever, and the washer-women and children are strewn along it the whole length of the town, as usual rubbing away from dawn until dark.

November 7.—Camp-news, talk of going to Tampico.

November 8.—At four o'clock this morning Theophilus Johnson died. We lamented his death though not so much as we would if we had not despaired of his recovery a week ago, and witnessed his sufferings; which we have reason to believe death has changed to joy. Inman is still weakly; this is a dusty windy day.

November 9.—Still dull, but warm sunshine in the day time and cool nights. The mesquites are shedding their leaves and most of the weeds have become hard and coarse. The gourds, watermelon and pumpkin vines are still growing as fresh as ever.

November 10.—I went out to cut wood today; we get fuel three miles south-east of town by cutting mesquite. We got some soft corn; at some fields where we were they were cutting corn, but roasting ears are getting scarce, though we saw some corn just getting in silk and tassel. Lots of asses.

November 11.—Ambrose Kenny died this morning. The funeral was at half past nine. His death was caused by measles; he and Johnson were buried in coffins, the first we could get since coming to Mexico. Kenny was a general favorite in the company. Not a word was said in the procession; the solemn movements bespoke sorrowful hearts; we smoothed the mound and returned to the quarters, but the countenance of everyone was changed, the stern soldiers who a moment before stood round the open grave of their companion, with sad countenance and heavy faces, had acquired cheerful appearances and jokes went around as lively as if death had never been with us. Such is the effect of war. A soldier becomes the football of passion; from grief to mirth or ambition, his life regarded as public property, as nothing, he is prepared to meet death or danger at any time and in any form.

November 12.—

"Swift are the feet of restless time
Hastening man to another clime."

November 13.—From day to day we have drill in the morning and evening, with cooking and eating between times. Our occupation is without variation.

November 14.—Orders to rub up our arms. David Bebee of this company died this morning. We think he died the death of the righteous as he appeared not to fear going; behind the curtain he was a young man of good disposition.

November 15.—This is a windy day and the dust is constantly flying about to annoy us in every form; we have to eat, cook, stand, sit, sleep and drill amid clouds of dust, and sand. A dry clear day.

November 16.—Half of this month gone. We paraded this evening in unform, marched to town formed in the square, went through the manual, then marched out to the third infantry, and was well pleased with their appearance. Dress parade with music.

November 17.—Another disagreeable day. Orders to move to Matamoros by water, consequently will leave as soon as we can get conveyance.

November 18.—Cloudy morning. There was a storm of wind and rain that came up very sudden this morning, while we had the tents down (this being Wednesday, the day for cleansing the encampment), that caused a good deal of confusion and trouble to pitch them again. The air became cool very sudden as quick as ever I saw in Illinois; the men are shivering about the fires, but in fine spirits, hoping their health will be better. Evening, a cool fresh breeze from the north.

November 19.—Last night was almost cool enough to frost; these mornings are cold but the days are sultry except when the wind blows, or the sun is obscured by clouds.

November 20.—The third regiment of Illinois Volunteers commenced drawing their pay today; they are shipping for Matamoros as fast as the boats can take them.

November 21.—We expect to leave this place in a few days, which we do not regret as it is a dull place. The town appears to have decayed from former note or greatness. Everything appears dull, the houses, the inhabitants little above savages and without energy or business of any importance going on. This appears to be caused by the want of commerce, with the indolence of the inhabitants and perhaps the want of a settled government that will secure property. But to bring about this change the country must be inhabited by a different race of people. The Spanish and Indian do not make a race of people with patriotism and candor enough to support a republic, much less to form, sustain and establish one out of the present deranged fabric called the Republic of Mexico.

November 22.—There was noise in the outskirts of town last night—four pistols were fired; then the noise of fighting succeeded. The guard was paraded and went to learn the cause; they found two men of the third regiment drunk who stated that they had been attacked by some Mexicans and had fired their pistols to raise the alarm. One of their number was missing, they supposed killed by the Mexicans. This morning the man was found lying in an alley, he had been stabbed in the side, ran there and laid until discovered this morning, his wound we fear is mortal. Today we saw the corpse of a boy who had died of the measles. They are very fatal at present among the Mexican children, who have caught them from the soldiers. Their funeral rites are Catholic.

November 23.—Cloudy this morning with appearance of rain; at noon clear, warm, windy and hot. Last night the man died who was stabbed the night previous. Last night there were two indifferent unoccupied houses burnt in town. This has been one of the most uncomfortable days I ever saw on account of wind and dust. There is orders for several of the companies to be ready to march at four o'clock in the morning, with one day's provisions.

November 24.—Two huts burnt last night. The men marched this morning at the appointed time. One Evans in Capt. Bishop's[42] company reported to headquarters yesterday evening that he has seen some sixty Mexicans and horses in a body five miles from here at a pond. But when the troops got there this morning they had turned into about thirty rangers.

[42] Captain William W. Bishop, Third Illinois Infantry.

November 25.—A light frost last night, high wind this evening.

November 26.—Nothing of importance.

November 27.—Commenced paying this regiment.

November 28.—Companies D, E, F, and B paid four months' wages and got on the *Tony* after dark.

November 29.—Started for Matamoros, lodged on a sand bar at two o'clock. A great many waded out to lighten the boat, got off, went down river, wooded, lay all night. The boys shot thirteen turkeys and some geese by moonlight.

November 30.—Left the shore at daylight. The *Corvette* passed us at nine while on a bar; Col. Baker got aboard of her, and we passed her again half a mile below on a bar. After encountering various difficulties, we tied up on the south side of the river; some of us went hunting on the other side of the river, but those on the side of the river where the boat lay shot five or six beeves yesterday. Two men were left by getting on shore to hunt, when she stopped to fix her rudder. Tied up at night a few miles above Old Reynosa.

December 1.—Put off from shore at daylight as usual. This is a warm rainy morning with purple clouds with golden edge stretching far away to the left of the sunrise, while he ascends the eastern horizon dimly shining, throwing an orange light about us. The wind increased to a perfect gale; the boat struggles on while countless flocks of wild geese start from the sand bars along the shore. Here and there a few prairie wolves prowling along the bank. Landed at Reynosa at four o'clock, staid for wind to fall. Reynosa is situated on the south side of river a quarter of a mile from it and sixty from Matamoros. It stands on a hill and has a neat appearance with good houses.

December 2.—On the river early, but soon got onto a

bar, stayed about six hours. Turkeys had been seen very plenty on the shore this morning and several of the boys went hunting, killed several turkeys, one hog and a goose or two. On the Texas side three hundred yards from the shore stands a cabin in which the boys found a box containing knives, forks and dishes and other delf[t] for the table. They also found augers, a hatchet, and other implements of American manufacture; besides books in Spanish, English, etc. There was stain on the wall like blood, and we supposed they had been murdered in the forepart of the summer. After getting supper then went down a mile or so and landed again on the Texas side. Went hunting again, shot a dozen or two turkey, three [rac]coons and some grouse or [prairie] chickens.

December 3.—Started at four o'clock, passed down the river. Winding around the bends of the river we scared up thousands of wild geese, saw turkeys in abundance, flocks of cranes, prairie wolves and plenty of cattle and horses. Landed at Matamoros at five P.M. Went to town, drank, made merry, returned to the boat, found that several had dipped too deep in strong drink, sailed about nine o'clock. Here Perryman was left. He and Skidmoore[43] of this company were taken out on patrols with the others to gather up stragglers, and did not get back in time to get on board.

December 4.—Landed at mouth at daylight. It is a cloudy showery morning. We cooked breakfast on shore, got off the boat with the baggage at ten o'clock. This is a pleasant place with balmy sea-air, boats, ships and various craft passing up or down the river, to Brazos or Point Isabel every now and then.

December 5.—James Henry's birthday. This is a fair, beautiful day. Colonel Baker passed through here on his

[43] Private Reuben Skidmore, Company E.

way to Washington.[44] We have plenty of fresh fish here. Inman takes them out of the river with line and hook. There is a good deal of business going on, building, etc.

December 6.—After breakfast this morning we prepared to return to Matamoros. We got on the *Whitesville* at twelve o'clock, left the shore, passed up the river, looking out on the flat swampy shores on each side of the river at the waterfowls. Four or five miles above the mouth we saw a large snake swimming across the river; it was seven or eight feet long and looked like a rattlesnake. This is not strange as the air is warm and pleasant, so much so that we bathed in the gulf while on the coast. Soon passed the old camp ground which looks very desolate as all the shades are gone and nothing present but the bleak hill where once stood the tangled thicket, then the pleasant grove with the long lines of tents animated by thousands of voices; but they are gone and nothing remains there but two solitary companies and they will leave in a few days. We left Beretee on the left and stopped a few miles above it.

December 7.—Left the shore early; nothing of importance occurred until two or three in the evening when the wind commenced blowing too hard for the boat to run; she tied up on the Texas side where there is a beautiful grove of palmetto trees carpeted with green grass. Here some of the boys went hunting and walked up to Matamoros, we landed there at seven or eight o'clock.

December 8.—Got the baggage on shore early this morning, pitched our tents with the regiment. It is northeast of Matamoros opposite Fort Brown, south of the river on a flat bottom that has been overflowed in the recent inundation; between here and town is a large pond of beautiful clear water; between the camp and the river is a battery or small

44 See notes 4 and 13 above.

fort built in a circular form to the height of eight or nine feet ditched around the outside; it was built by the Mexicans in the defense of the place. From it they annoyed Major Brown.

December 9.—This is a cool airy morning. We resumed the drill as usual. We buried one out of the third regiment, he formerly belonged to Co. B, but was discharged on account of his health; he died in a few hours after getting aboard the boat to sail for the mouth. Lieut. McNeil[45] attended the funeral with some of his company.

December 10.—Very cool morning. We were ordered to hold ourselves in readiness to march at twenty-four hours' warning; we are to take one tent to eight men, three camp kettles to a company; the rest of the baggage is to be sent around to Tampico by water. We are ordered to prepare for a review at nine A.M. This and the third regiment and third Ohio, also Tennessee cavalry to be reviewed, before the quarters of the third regiment Illinois Vol. at twelve o'clock tomorrow.

December 11.—Passed the review in compliance to the orders of yesterday. The four regiments made a grand appearance, the cavalry looked splended, the horses are far superior to the Mexican breed and are in fine shape. There are a great many of the troops corned[46] this evening.

December 12.—This morning the steamboat *Troy* passed up the river carrying some regular troops; mostly new recruits just from the States.

December 13.—This is a rainy day but warm and pleasant.

December 14.—All is hurry, bustle, and confusion this morning as it is the appointed time to march; while packing

[45] First Lieutenant W. L. McNeil, Third Illinois Infantry.

[46] Intoxicated.

up Cowel[47] of this company and one Davis of Company C had a fight which we consider no credit to either of them. We packed up in compliance to orders by joining with four others: W. Lowry, W. Whelis, W. Reny and T. Hutchens,[48] for Inman being in bad health we had to leave him behind with several others to go around by water, so after loading the baggage in the wagons we parade marched into town and stacked our arms in the square (dismissed) ten minutes. At the beat of the drums we assumed our places in the line, took up the line of march, accompanied by the third regiment and some of the cavalry with the wagons and camped at night six miles from town beside a lake.[49] This is a beautiful place for an encampment being set with fine grass studded over with clumps of bushes like a close set peach orchard carpeted with blue grass and the lake or pond spread out on one side with bushes growing every here and there, out of the silver sheet of water which reflected a thousand stars while the croaking of frogs completed the music of the scene and lullabied every soldier to sleep.

December 15.—Awoke this morning at beat of reveille and commenced getting breakfast, this is a very pleasant morning—the fog and smoke hangs over the camp with a

[47] Private Samuel Cornell.

[48] See the reference to eight men in the entry for December 10. Their mess probably constituted Sergeant William Lowry, Corporal William Kinney, Private Isaac W. Whillis, and Thomas Hutchins, as well as James Henry, James Perryman, James Inman, and Thomas Tennery.

[49] The Third and Fourth Illinois Infantry and the Tennessee Cavalry regiments marched to Ciudad Victoria (capital of the state of Tamaulipas) by way of Santa Teresa and San Fernando under General Patterson (see note 53 below). Another column moved from Camargo under Quitman, and a third from Monterrey under Taylor. They converged at Victoria. Tampico had meanwhile been taken by Colonel Coffee's Alabama Regiment and by an artillery force under General Shields, with navy help.

gloomy appearance but all is life, joy and merriment with the soldiers. Breakfast over, we paraded for the road, in the meantime the third regiment put into the lake, whooping like so many Indians. This soon ceased and the splashing of the water rattled like a summer breeze sweeping over a field of green corn; but we had not long to listen for ere they had got far, our front was in. We crossed this lake, it being half-leg deep and a quarter of a mile wide, then we stopped to put on our shoes for most of the men had drawn them off preparatory to the wade; then we took up the march through the chaparral on a dim road and traveled about six miles. There are holes in the ground like sink-holes made in the ground by water running under ground, they are from one to three feet deep. After marching six miles we came to a creek or small river called the Rio del Tigre. This is a running stream but very low at present. After marching near four miles we came to a prairie or wet plain where we turned to the left and travelled two miles then crossed an outlet of a pond and camped between it and the above named stream; within the last two [miles] we killed two large black snakes. This encampment is located on a beautiful rise of ground, the prairie spread far way to the west, interspersed with ponds while countless numbers of mules, horses and cattle may be seen grazing on it; there is no scarcity of waterfowl here neither. The stream is about two hundred yards east of the encampment.

December 16.—This is another beautiful day. The men appear in fine spirits, good health and lively; we cleared off a parade ground and prepared sinkers[50] as if intending to stay for some time. There was a large blue colored snake killed today between this and the creek. It appeared harmless, there being no poisonous fangs in its mouth. It was

[50] Probably cesspools—an English usage of the word.

about three inches in diameter through the body and six feet long.

December 17.—Nothing today more than is common; the Mexicans brought some mustangs in to sell; they sell ponies from six to ten dollars apiece.[51]

December 18.—Mr. Hite and Lt. Maltby went back to Matamoros today to lay in some provisions or notions preparatory to the march. The fore part of this day has been very warm but there is an uncommon cool evening, the changes of temperature being very sudden. James Perryman is unwell this evening with the diarrhea, this complaint has been running on him ever since he left Camargo.

December 19.—Hite and Maltby returned this evening bringing the unwelcome news that Job Clifton[52] was dead. He died the next day after we left. His brother deeply mourned his loss. Alas this is not all but there is a widow at home where ties were stronger than brother, sister, father or mother. Such are the chances of fate and a soldier should always be prepared for death or life without a moment's warning.

December 20.—This is the Sabbath, no drill. There are a great many Mexicans about the camp, running horses over the parade ground. There are some packs of oranges for sale a mile south of here. They were fetched there on mules by Mexicans traders from the interior.

December 21.—A fair day, after a cool night. This evening we paraded as usual for drill, but marched down the stream to where the Matamoros road crosses it with the intention

51 Many infantrymen bought ponies to ride. They were called the "Mustang Cavalry."

52 Evidently a brother of Private William Clifton of Company E. Job is recorded on the roster of Company E as having died at Matamoros on December 18, 1846.

of meeting General Patterson[53] but he did not arrive; at dark two pieces of artillery came up with some wagons that stopped on the other side of the river.

December 22.—Beautiful morning; the wagons continued to come in all day. At twelve o'clock it commenced raining and rained about two hours. Patterson arrived in company with the cavalry while it was raining. After the rain we moved our tents to the creek bank to get out of the mud and water which was two or three inches deep. On the river are encamped some [men] out of almost every company in

[53] Major General Robert Patterson was born in Ireland in 1792, the son of an Irish revolutionary who fled to America in 1798. He engaged in the family mercantile trade in Tennessee and Pennsylvania. During the War of 1812 he joined the Pennsylvania militia (rising from captain to colonel) and later the U.S. Army, in which he served as a first lieutenant and captain. After 1815 he returned to business but remained active in the Pennsylvania militia and by the mid-1830's was the senior major general. It was in this rank that he was called to active duty in July, 1846. He was, next to General Scott, the highest-ranking officer in the army. Taylor put under Patterson's command all the troops assembling on the Río Grande, at one time numbering about twelve thousand. After leading a third of these troops overland to Ciudad Victoria and Tampico, Patterson joined Scott to reconnoiter Veracruz. At the siege of Veracruz, Patterson commanded one of the three divisions of the army, the other two being led by Pillow and Worth. Although he was too ill to lead his troops at Cerro Gordo, he left his sickbed to be present at the battle. Scott had no command suitable to Patterson's rank when the first volunteer regiments went home, and Patterson was therefore placed in charge of the rear echelon, moving supplies and reinforcements from Veracruz to the front lines.

Patterson and William Orlando Butler were the two major generals of volunteers. Butler served in the War of 1812, when he rose to captain and was breveted major for gallantry at the Battle of New Orleans (Congress voted him a sword for his part in the Battle of Monterrey). It was Butler who marched to Ciudad Victoria to meet the other two columns. Major General William J. Worth, a regular (also voted a sword for Monterrey), was left in command at Saltillo. General Wool, then the senior brigadier general in the army, was left in command at Parras. He was later to be breveted major general and awarded a sword for his part in the Battle of Buena Vista.

the regiment. This is a beautiful night as the clouds are retiring to the south, leaving the northern horizon dotted over with millions of silver gems. The air is warm enough to be comfortable. The stream glides silently along shaded with bushes and enlivened by the croaking of frogs. The men standing around the fires drying themselves; in the meantime, repeating old stories and shaking their sides at the same time; the impudent but cowardly prairie wolf chattering two or three hundred yards from us; all, in sweet confusion, sought the shade.

December 23.—Colonel Forman's regiment started from this place with part of the cavalry and artillery. We are to start in the morning being one day in the rear.

December 24.—During the roll of the reveille we arose, and commenced preparing breakfast and packing knapsacks and so forth. At eight o'clock we paraded ready to march. The adjutant announced Mr. Hite sergeant quartermaster in place of Wenters[54] who was discharged, and delivered the regiment to the major.[55] We started in a southern direction varying to the south; after marching about a mile we came to prairie. After marching twelve miles we halted at a ranch between two ponds, a part of the cavalry is here. The third regiment lay here last night.

December 25.—Early this morning we arose and prepared to start soon after sunrise. Soon the long line of cavalry led off, then the wagons next came, our motley troops, some on horseback, others straggling out of their companies; still behind us were the largest portion of the wagons and the guard which brought up the rear. Our line lay through open prairie on which are hundreds of wild horses or rather shy

[54] See note 1 above. Gilbert E. Winter was twice appointed and reduced in rank.

[55] Major Thomas L. Harris.

mustangs claimed by the Mexicans. After marching four or five miles we came to some sloughy or low places in which are ponds and puddles of water salty as brine, in these are crabs of enormous size, around these ponds there is crystallized salt two or three inches deep and as transparent as ice. After marching about twelve miles we halted, opened [ground] on the left of the road and got some muddy water, then left and marched about as far again and halted at a place called Santa Teresa. This is a ranch of some note; we got water from pools made in the branch by digging holes in the ground three or four yards across and as many deep to hold water in a dry time. The ground in this encampment is rough and uneven; this has been a Christmas long to be remembered as we have marched about twenty-four miles and are very tired.

December 26.—Fatiguing has been this day's march. We left the encampment early as usual, and marched through a level prairie with large herds of horses grazing on it; about nine o'clock we came in sight of the mountains far away to the southwest, they appear bluer than the sky in summer. A red deer ran through between two companies about noon. We passed a pond on the left of the road. [It was] all the water that we passed today, even it was not fit to drink, as there was a dead mustang in it, in addition to being thick with mud. We met some Mexicans with mules packed with oranges. They relieved us very much; they cost us six and a fourth cents apiece. No language can describe this day's march as it really was, we marched nearly thirty miles without water for man or beast, at night we can get only half a pint of muddy water each, and have to lay on the bare ground,[56] without tents; for supper we have some roasting

[56] Of this march Farber says: "The Illinoisans were great chaps for soldiers; full of fun and life, enduring any fatigue, and making sport of

ears to eat, quite a novelty to Illinoisians at this time of year. The price is six and one-fourth [cents] for three. We have come to broken land, the water is drawn from a well.

December 27.—Great as was the day's march yesterday, we had nine miles to march before breakfast this morning. We got up and started almost without orders, everyone as he chose or rather as he could. In about five miles we came to where some of the cavalry were encamped at some ranches in a valley or low place where there is plenty of water in wells; after watering and resting we started on, marching over stony roads until we came in sight of San Fernando. It is on a rise close to a river of the same name. This town has a handsome appearance being built mostly of limestone and the walls plastered with cement. There is plenty of sour oranges growing in this place; the gardens are enclosed with stone. The town cemetery is east of it, and enclosed by a stone wall nine feet high with doors or gateways in each side. At the east side, in the centre, is a square in the wall which bears the same proportion to the lot as a fireplace does to a square room, at the entrance of which is placed on each side paintings after the Catholic fashion. There are crosses on the wall every eight or ten feet apart. There are a few tombs in this place plastered with cement but the most common way is to bury without coffins and pack the dirt in hard on the corpse; in digging the grave they dig up a great many skeletons. In the southeast corner is a large pile of bones of all sizes; everywhere that a hole is left in the side of the wall there are placed skulls facing to the front; some of them are fresh dug-up and appearing as if they had not

it; splendid in discipline and military precision of evolution; and afterwards when occasion required, they fought most bravely" (*The Twelve Month Volunteer*). (Farber later played a prominent role in the Idaho gold rush of 1861–62. The rich and famous Camp Florence was named for his daughter.)

been long dead. In this place are two vaults under a stone arch about nine feet high, supported by four pillars: these stand at the corners, the arch crossing in the middle. Leaving this we went through the town to the river; this stream has a swift running current of cool clear water. We encamped south of town in a bottom.

December 28.—Half of the brigade crossed the river in the morning and the other half in the evening; the bank on the opposite being very steep, it was very hard to get up the wagons. We waded the stream, being over knee deep. As we started, a Mexican stole two wagon tongues and was caught and was made to carry them over the river to the new encampment, where a sergeant and two privates were ordered to give him two kicks which they did.

December 29.—In the morning before day we arose early with the intention of starting at daylight which we did, marching south over stony roads with hills in view in every direction; after marching twenty-one miles or so, we came to this river or large creek and crossed it; the water is bracking the banks of sand where it dries, being impregnated with saline.

December 30.—Journeying is always fatiguing; we found ourselves on the road early as usual advancing over a rough way, crossing a deep ravine about nine o'clock. There is a lofty range of mountains far to the left. About five in the afternoon I left the road on the right and went down in a low place and killed a wild turkey. Finally after marching twenty-three miles we halted at a branch where there is plenty of water running from springs; two or three wagons turned over within the last three miles; several mules gave out today.

December 31.—Queen of the night had not hid behind the western hills ere the reveille called the sleeping soldiers to duty. We started as soon as it was light, marching on a dry level road about four miles; this is almost a water level. In various places there are dry ponds. At the brink of this there is a spring coming out of the bank near the top and falling into the wide spread valley to the depth of one hundred feet. From this bluff we can see the village of San Tanda,[57] a distance of eight miles. This village lies on the northeast side of the river or mountain stream and a quarter of a mile from it. The town is a fine little village for Mexico, and contains a church burying ground and so forth, but is worthy of note on the account of a stone dam across the above named stream; this dam is built of stone to the height of seven feet with an apron below this, and ten stone braces besides strong buttments on each side. This is to water the town, there being a small canal running from the pond through the town all the time. The dam is built of rough stone but plastered with cement and paved and [so well] erected that I think that it far exceeds anything of the kind I ever saw before. We crossed the river a little below the dam and camped on the bank. The water is the best we have had.

[57] Santander.

1847

January 1.—Long as a year appears in the future, we can look back to the last new year as if it had been yesterday. What a change has taken place in the last short year we all can now see. The coming long years to us may never be. Travelled about ten miles and camped at a well with a cistern of stone work at it, twenty by eighteen feet square, and a trough running from it for stock with a wall between them; the hole is cemented or plastered complete with lime that shows a master's skill in masonry. The water has formerly been raised through a hole in the cistern by animal power.

January 2.—Moving early as usual over some of the stoniest roads I ever saw. There are some tall mountains to the right. After twelve miles' march we came to a two story house[1] built of stone and plastered fresh that gave it a fine appearance. Part of the house is old and appears as if it had stood for centuries. Near to this place is a creek called San Antonio. The stream runs in a deep ravine; there is cypress and ash growing along the edge of the water, the first we have seen in this country.

[Later.] With a good deal of work, we crossed the stream and pitched tents. One of Co. K killed a peccary, a kind

[1] The hacienda of San Antonio.

of hog peculiar to America. It is said at the above named house that the Emperor Iturbide was slain.

January 3.—Night had not been succeeded by daylight, until one hundred of the regiment was detailed to help the remaining part of the train over the river. After marching three miles we came to the San Antonio river, a broad beautiful swift stream, knee deep on the riffles. On the banks large willows and cypress are growing. In a quarter of a mile, we came to a village of poor appearance.[2] Near night some of us killed two turkeys. They are quite plentiful and tame. After dark we came to the camp, after crossing a creek at the end of seven leagues' march.

January 4.—On the road one hour before day, passed through a small village[3] with a large looking church. Marched twenty miles and arrived at Victory[4] which is near the mountains. This is a good looking town, to be on the plaza with a stream running around the west side. We camped below the town in a corn field.

January 5.—Passed a cool night in camp; frost on the fine straw this morning. There are beautiful green parrots flying about here. There are more than two thousand soldiers in this vicinity, Taylor and Quitman's divisions being here.[5] General Taylor visited our encampment this evening. He is a heavy set, corpulent and old looking man.

2 Padilla.

3 Actually another hacienda.

4 Ciudad Victoria (see note 49 above). The city, with a population of about eight thousand at the time, had been named for Guadalupe Victoria, hero of the Mexican wars of independence and first president of the Republic of Mexico.

5 A conservative estimate; there were about two thousand in Tennery's column alone. Quitman had taken possession of the city five days before, and Taylor had reached the city earlier on the same day that Tennery's regiment arrived.

January 6.—Round the south and east of this place are hills. Out south is a small one which I ascended today, and overlooked the whole country. We can see the creek winding around the town, with patches of green corn or sugar cane here and there; also the beautiful stone wall around the graveyard, and different encampments and ranches up and down the stream.

January 7.—A squall of wind struck the encampment last night; it blew over nearly all the tents. This is a very cool windy day with thin clouds. There is ice a quarter of an inch thick in the water vessels this morning.

January 8.—There were some of the boys out hunting today, and found some snow under a shrub, three or four miles south of here. Several deer have been brought in. Ice again on the water vessels this morning. Celebrated the day by marching out and firing one round of blank cartridge.

January 9.—Up as usual this morning. Struck tents at eleven to march to General Quitman's brigade,[6] to which we are attached for the remaining part of the campaign. Paraded at eleven o'clock, and started, passed through the town. The west side is the best part of the place. After marching about one mile from town, we passed a stone wall five feet high on the right of the road. This is the encampment of our brigade. The fence [wall] above-named, more than a mile long, runs between the enclosure of a rich planter and the road. The creek runs through these posses-

[6] Brigadier General John A. Quitman was born in New York in 1798, studied law in Ohio, and then moved to Natchez, Mississippi. There he practiced law and served in both houses of the legislature and as acting governor in 1835–36. In 1836 he took part in the Texas Revolution. As a brigadier general under Taylor he won distinction at Monterrey, and was promoted to major general on April 14, 1847. He fought under Scott at Veracruz and Puebla and took part in the storming of Chapultepec. Scott appointed him to serve as governor of Mexico City during the occupation.

sions, and there are ditches running all over the plantation wherever needed, full of fresh cool running water.

January 10.—Valuable as the Sabbath is, we have to clean up the encampment today: this we finished at ten o'clock. We went down to the sugar cane: this grows in rows two feet apart with ridges eighteen inches high between them. The cane tassels in this country which it seldom does in the States. There is a large sugar manufactory on this farm. This is a very cold day for this country.

January 11.—West of us on top of the mountain there are some clouds which look like fog rising from the river. This is another cool day. Nothing of importance going on today.

January 12.—Nothing today, no drill or parade. Warmer than yesterday.

January 13.—Just after sunrise, Lieutenant Murphy,[7] Corporal [William] Davis, [Private Samuel] Cowell [Cornell] and myself started for the mountains. After crossing the sugar farm and passing along a path about a mile in length, we began to ride up the ridges. Just as we began to climb we saw a flock of turkeys in a ravine. Davis shot at one and Cornell flashed at another. We resumed our journey, a constant ascent upward and still upward. At length we halted to rest and could look back to the plain below, to see numerous plantations here and there and the creek where it left the mountains, with its various wanderings for miles along the plain. Also another [stream runs] four or five miles to the south, which forms a junction with this one several miles below, and the different sized improvements. The town and all the streets, alleys, etc., in fact, all the country can be seen like a map. Again we started; our path

[7] First Lieutenant Richard Murphy, Company E, Fourth Illinois Infantry. He is listed as a private on the roster but as a first lieutenant in the *Historical Register*.

continued to increase in steepness, over rocks, sometimes supporting ourselves by holding to bushes or clinging to crags of the rocks. We gained the top of a narrow ridge, where had we fallen we should not have stopped short of several hundred feet. Leaving the ridge we passed across the head of a hollow, two or three rods deep, and again began to climb steeps, more difficult than ever. At length we began to reach the top region. Here is growing a species of oak which looks like burr-oak, they are about eighteen inches through on an average, and thirty feet high. When on top we sat down and ate dinner of biscuit and sugar. We can see peaks still higher, to the north-west, and far to the east across the plain there are mountains, a peak of which is higher than any in this vicinity.[8] After finishing our meal we started to return, the Lieutenant and Davis the same way we went up. Cornell and myself coming down a hollow, this we found more difficult than the other way, as we had to climb down many places where we were in imminent danger of loosing our hold and being dashed to pieces, hundreds of feet below. After encountering many difficulties, we again got back to encampment, after dark, hungry and tired but satisfied with the trip.

January 14.—Lieutenant Ross[9] came up today from Matamoros with the provision train, bringing dispatches from General Scott,[10] who is at Matamoros, also letters belonging to this regiment from the States. This is a warm pleasant day. A riot between Co. F and Mexicans.

January 15.—Orders to march in the morning. Duck John

[8] The Tamaulipas Mountains.

[9] First Lieutenant Leonard F. Ross, Company K, Fourth Illinois Infantry.

[10] Major General Winfield Scott, commanding general, U.S. Army, who was to lead the invasion forces from Veracruz to Mexico City.

of Co. A killed a panther and brought in its tail. Dress parade at 4 P.M.

January 16.—Reveille at four. Started soon after, we marched into town, halted while the dragoons and artillery passed us, then started and marched through the Plaza, out at the south side of town across the branch, then along a dry bed. A mile or so out we passed or rather crossed a rill of good cold water and a pond to the left of the road. After marching fifteen miles on a level road with larger timber than usual on each side of it, we came to this place. Here is a beautiful little brook, with plenty of trout, gurgling from rock to rock, as it flows from the mountains to the gulf. Along its banks are growing sycamores, pecans and gum with all other sorts of timber common along streams in this country.

January 17.—Our road lies through a level country with ridges here and there and an occasional ravine with water. Co. C's wagon broke down today. We have come fifteen miles today on an easterly course, and are camped on a small brook, with the mountain several miles to the south.

January 18.—We marched in front of the brigade today, along a level road with ridges on the side; we stopped close to a hill on the left of the road. The general and staff went up on it to look back at the troops. We came to a branch[11] close to the above named ridge, and halted to stay for the night. I went up the ridge; it appears to be level or nearly so, back west and overlooks the valley. There is a beautiful stretch of grass along the branch four or five hundred yards from it. There are no ranches or habitations near.

January 19.—This is a chilly, lonesome morning. We marched southeast along a level dusty road until we came to

[11] This stream, also referred to in the entries for January 19 and 21 is the Río del Limón, also called the Río Forlón.

a small village fifteen miles from the camp. One mile back we passed over a damp piece of road, everywhere else being dry and dusty. On the other side of town is a large bold running stream, which we crossed and travelled down six miles. In about three miles we met contractor Biglow. He was wounded in the leg. He was attacked by some Mexicans, while returning from Pillow's[12] division, but outran them by having a good horse.

January 20.—In about a mile after we left camp, we crossed the river Polto. There is a ranch on this side. The river is a swift running stream and has flood marks forty feet high. On this side the river is a level ridge covered with large beautiful palm trees. We passed about eleven miles of beautiful green grass with palm trees forty feet high. Leaving this we came to an old building of stone one story high, built of stone and two hundred feet long.[13] Just after leaving this we crossed a branch and followed the road for about seven miles over rolling country, covered with a species of timber like pecan. We are encamped on a branch where there is larger timber than usual and prickly pears with red blooms.

January 21.—We left the encampment early and marched nine miles, and came to a town with a large Plaza and church with steeple,[14] and statues in front. Leaving this we marched eleven miles more and camped at a branch close to a village. This day's march has been over a beautiful country with ridges of mountains far to the left. Early this

[12] General Gideon J. Pillow, born in Tennessee in 1808, was James K. Polk's law partner. He was appointed brigadier general of volunteers on July 1, 1846, and was promoted to major general on April 13, 1847. He served at the battles of Veracruz, Cerro Gordo, and Chapultepec.

[13] The hacienda of Alamita.

[14] The hacienda of Chocoi.

morning we saw a spike or rock far to the fore.[15] When we came several miles nearer we discovered it was far to the right of the road. This peak is quite a curiosity. It stands on a high hill, and appears to be about a hundred yards thick and twice as high; from the top of the hill it appears to be rock with crags and fissures from top to bottom, and appears to be a part of the ancient pillars of time that has withstood convulsions of the earth until the once high mountains around it have been shaken down and become a level plain, for there are many traces of earthquakes in this country.

January 22.—Left the encampment, our company with "I" being rear guard. We marched about six miles over beautiful rolling prairie with chaparral here and there. About eleven o'clock a few Mexican travellers caught up with us. They were very much frightened, and stated that there were Mexican soldiers behind us. At this information, a few horsemen rode back and saw some mounted men, who fled at their approach. In about two hours we came to a large ranch. Here is a pond saved by a dam. At this place the rolls were called, and there are two men missing, one by the name of Thomas Rudder out of Co. I, the other from the Baltimore battalion. Traveled sixteen miles. The pillar of rock which we passed yesterday is still in sight, and appears of a different shape as we are on another side.

January 23.—We marched sixteen miles today mostly over broken land, with ridges in view far to the right and left of the road. The road lay mostly through chaparral, and on a dead hollow stub about twenty feet high, we saw an animal of the lizard kind of a dirty black color, about three feet long. At the camp of the twentieth we saw one dead; the fire had run over it. It was about the same size, and had teeth something like an alligator. The cavalry went back

[15] Mount Bernal.

this morning, and found one man dead that answered the description of Rudder, two leagues from this place: he had been shot through the breast and stabbed twice. We are encamped at some ranches close to a pond at present.

January 24.—Some of the soldiers of a Georgia regiment got some mescal or Mexican whiskey from the ranches last night; they are very merry today. The road is pretty much the same as yesterday, but more rolling and prairie. The men amuse themselves by gathering pods of a sort of fruit that grows on a briery flag and sucking the juice from it. There are many things for a naturalist to study in this country, both animal and vegetable. There are prickly pears of every variety growing from the tops of the mountains to the lowest levels, out of rocks, without earth or scarcely a crack for the root, or on top of the grass covered roofs, and I saw one of the broad kind growing out of a live standing palm tree. There are also grasses of a coarse thick bladed kind, red and green, growing in little tufts upon the branches of the bushes something as mistletoe does, though the roots grow round the limbs instead of in them, consequently the grass must take all of its nourishment from the atmosphere using the roots only as supports. And various kinds of timber for which I have no name. We saw green corn today in silk and tassel a few miles from this place. Marched eighteen miles today and came to the encampment at Elmeto.[16] This is a fine looking place and contains a church. There is a lake[17] or bay that runs from here to the gulf. It is very shallow and has many islands and green spots in it.

January 25.—Cloudy this morning. Left the camp and marched about three miles and camped again on the lake shore. This little march has been through woods with trees

[16] Altamira.

[17] Lake Carpentero.

larger than usual. We passed a burning coal pit, and saw where two more had been burned, the first thing of the kind we have seen in Mexico. There is live oak and many other kinds of timber growing here with long branches and short trunks, forming dark tangled thickets. There is a kind of wood growing here with vine like trunks or roots growing round other trees to the top, then united into a body out of which grows branches; thus they form an unnatural top to many large trees.

January 26.—Another cloudy morning, but a warm sultry day. When the sun came out warm about nine o'clock, an alligator about five feet long crawled up out of a bunch of grass and some of the men snapped a pistol at it, which made it take to the water again. There have been several Mexicans with canoes or large dugouts, loaded with bread, sweet potatoes and spirits for sale. Down below here on this side of the lake, there is plenty of soft white limestone, bedded two or three feet deep, overgrown with timber. There is a small farm a half mile below with corn waist high and sweet potatoes growing among it; they run all over the ground, with roots all along the vines. There are also lettuce, onions and tomatoes growing here, the first we have seen in the country. We heard that Lieut. Post[18] is at Tampico and all the men except Inman are well.

January 27.—Mr. Hite went to town. After breakfast I went down to the other brigade. The road lay over uneven ground of groves and swamps. They are encamped in a field; there is a grocery in a good house at this place. Two hundred yards below this encampment is a banyan tree with about fifty trunks, the bark is white and smooth but soft, and when cut it oozes out a milk colored sap. After looking at this, I,

[18] Second Lieutenant John P. Post, Company C, Fourth Illinois Infantry.

with two more men went to see another, it stands a mile further off and is twice as large as the other. These trees have a leaf like an orange, and tender branches without thorns. In going to the above named tree, we travelled along several ponds on the banks of which lay plenty of perriwinkles an inch and a half long and large in proportion, of a dark color. Along this path close to the large banyan we saw a large track, I supposed it to be the trail of a bear. In a dry pond close to that place one of the men shot at a large deer. Mr. Hite has returned and informed us that he saw Lieut. Post and all the men are with him save Inman, he was left at the point [Isabel] in the hospital.

January 28.—Struck our tents at sunrise and started for Tampico. In about a mile, after passing the encampment of Pillow's brigade, our road lay over deep sand, on each side of which is one dark thicket for four miles. Then we came to uneven or broken land, spread over with scattered ranches and large timber. After marching three miles more we camped in an old field on the right of the road. In the fields along this road, patches of green corn and sugar cane are growing, the corn is in tassle.

January 29.—Got leave of the captain and went to town. It is built on a high point that extends out into the bay. The buildings are of stone, and are mostly covered with tiling. The streets are paved with stone and have a healthy appearance. The market is very good being supplied with almost every variety of vegetable grown in the temperate or torrid zone. After looking round through the city we came round by the camp of Lieutenant Post and the boys, they came out with us to camp.

January 30.—This camp is on a ridge that extends out to the west of the road and overlooks an arm of the bay that extends from town to a great distance southwest of this place. In fact all the lowlands in this vicinity are subject to overflow, and the hills for many leagues back appear to have been built by the boisterous waves of the Gulf, as they are formed of fossil shells and sand mingled with gravel or soft limestone. As I said, this encampment overlooks the bay; that is, we can look across the widespread bay far to the west, with its green groves and rushes in all their loveliness.

January 31.—A cloudy day with broken clouds floating about and a few drops of rain.

February 1.—This was a cloudy morning but faired off about twelve. Almost all the trees are green, and the birds are hopping from branch to branch in search for food or frolicksome pastime, while their beautiful chattering notes lend much to the day, and call men's minds to behold their beautiful plumage. The first or most noted is the green parrot, with yellow head and red shoulders. This bird is a third larger than the pigeon and is constantly flying from place to place in company with each other. Connubial love seems to be very strong with these birds, as they always fly in pairs, though they sometimes associate several pairs together, for the sake of sociability. Next is the jay or a large black bird with a yellow beak and the habits of the jay, though it is larger than a blackbird. It has the shape and voice of the jay and a white breast. Third there is a little green parakeet, beside the red bird, and a yellow kind with black shoulders; also the mocking, the cow blackbird, thrush and wren besides several other kinds. They call the attention of the curious, render a subject for study to the naturalist, and display the beauties of nature, and the wisdom of its author who gave them instinct to retire from heat or cold, changing their residence from clime to clime, over lakes and seas, and rearing their young at the best and most convenient season of the year for food and protection.

February 2.—Another beautiful day added to the many that we have passed in this country; just after dark there are clouds in the west with lightning.

February 3.—Near to twelve o'clock some Mexicans came and informed General Shields that there were robbers on the road a few miles back of this place. He detailed thirty men and went to ascertain if it were the fact. When he got nearly to the place, being a little ways in front of the guard, he sent the Mexicans ahead to see if they would be attacked. When the robbers halted them and were about to commence pillaging, Shields made his appearance. They fled into the chaparral before the detail came up. Then the general sent some in search of them, others to paths where he thought they would be most likely to pass, and orders for four hundred men, two hundred from each regiment to guard the road and search the woods, but we could not find them. A guard was then placed by the way to detect them if possible.

February 4.—Our arms were inspected by Shields and aide. Company drill at nine A.M. and regimental at four P.M.

February 5.—The sick that were left at Matamoros are coming in. Dr. Cass[19] and several others came out from town. Col. Baker and Moore landed at town.[20] Moore has come to camp since dark. [Private] William Clifton is the only one of this company that has come; he is fresh and hearty.

[19] Possibly Dr. Alexander M. Cassidy, First Pennsylvania Infantry.

[20] Baker, the regimental commander, had just returned from the trip to Washington to obtain supplies and clothing for his men. Lieutenant Colonel John Moore was Baker's second-in-command.

February 6.—Colonel Baker came out from town this morning. The meeting with him and Moore both is joy for the regiment. Baker has brought clothing for the regiment. The third regiment boys have been making a new kind of sport, for me, by shaving and greasing a pig, then letting it go for the one that catches it to keep. But among the joy we have reasons for grief, for again the doleful death march has sounded in our ears. This is the funeral of Henry Maury of Co. I.[21] A shower of rain last night.

February 7.—This day has been employed in drawing and distributing clothing to the men.

February 8.—This day has been taken up like yesterday.

February 9.—A warm cloudy morning, policing or cleaning quarters. Just after dark there were clouds in the south that emitted lightning.

February 10.—A cool windy day. At this time I am suffering with a toothache. I attribute it to cold. Alas there is another of our soldiers left the stage of action, one Wallace, a brother to Lieutenant [William] Wallace,[22] that died at Camargo of Co. B. He was buried by the side of Maury. There they lay like warriors taking their rest, no more to be roused by the reveille or to suffer on the toilsome march of this life's journey, or their pulse to beat high in ambition's path nor to run low at the approach of Lethe's shadow. But they lie and sweetly sleep beneath the shade of the groves where leaves are always green and flowers fresh, where the howling gulf will lullaby their ashes, while her waves heave and winds waft our vessels from clime to clime.

February 11.—Still cool and cloudy. Henry and I walked

[21] Henry McGarvey, one of the two surviving brothers referred to in the entry for July 11, 1846. The third brother was Francis McGarvey.

[22] First Lieutenant Andrew J. Wallace, Company B, Fourth Illinois Infantry.

out east of the encampment and saw limes and lemons under some trees that stood in a row in an old uncultivated field. There is a great deal of open land around here that has been cultivated but is now grown up in small growth timber.

February 12.—Rained all last night. Lieut. Murphy, Private McDeed and myself went out from the camp, and got two chickens and six eggs for which we paid seventy-five cents. Coming back we saw an animal about the size of a grey fox of a brown color. This evening I went out to get wood and fetched in a stump which I put on the fire, and there came from under the bark of it a green snake, four feet long and only as thick as my finger, it was active and, when irritated, vicious, but I do not think poisonous.

February 13.—Cloudy, pleasant day.

February 14.—Belford[23] of this Company died at the hospital. This being Valentine's day no doubt the young folks at home are employing it in making love, or visiting, or receiving company, and making merry, which we think is the duty of all nature to enjoy the time as well as possible, and stick to virtue.

February 15.—This morning great roaring of cannons in Tampico.[24] We were amazed at things of this kind; we heard of making a parade ground as if we were to stay here some time.[25] We buried Owen Belford this evening. The corpse being brought and placed in the quarters, the musicians collected and the escort ready. As we raised the coffin the music began the dead march, followed by the firing party, then the pall bearers, followed by the company. Thus

23 Private Owen Belford is recorded as having died at Tampico on February 14, 1847.

24 The artillery salute for General Scott upon his arrival at Tampico.

25 Owing to a shortage of transport, they remained for another three weeks.

we proceeded to the open grave, lowered the coffin, fired the farewell, filled the grave and raised a mound and left.

February 16.—Damp morning, drilled by Gen. Shields, nearly all day. A large mail came in but nothing for me, which I am out of humor about. Captain Rolstand's[26] Co. went to town to bury Capt. Morris,[27] who died yesterday.

February 17.—I was on guard last night; it was about as cool as June in Illinois. The fireflies were floating about in the air, emitting their electric flashes. The sun arose clear and beautiful to dispel the dews. A warm beautiful day.

February 18.—Hard thunder in the south last night. We were drilled by Gen. Shields' aide.

February 19.—Passed a review before Twiggs[28] today. Many of the troops are preparing to embark to Vera Cruz.

February 20.—Received two months' pay.

February 21.—Commenced raining about ten o'clock and continued until near three this morning. This is a warm day. The rain last night was accompanied with lightning and loud thunder.

February 22.—Five of this company went to town. On the right of the road about two hundred yards from it, in the encampment cleared off by Twiggs' division, stand two or three mounds ten to fifteen feet high, as monuments of that

26 Perhaps Captain Lewis W. Ross, Company K, Fourth Illinois Infantry. There is no record of a Captain Rolstand in the Mexican War.

27 Captain Achilles Morris, Company D, Fourth Illinois Infantry, who died at Tampico on February 15, 1847, and was succeeded by Second Lieutenant Alfred C. Campbell.

28 General David E. Twiggs was born in 1790 and served as a captain in the War of 1812. He later fought in the Seminole and Black Hawk wars. Serving as a colonel under Taylor, he so distinguished himself at Palo Alto and Resaca de la Palma that he was promoted to brigadier general in June, 1846. Transferred to Scott's command, he fought at Veracruz and led the van in the march on Mexico City, at Cerro Gordo, Contreras, and Churubusco.

once numerous race that spread over this continent, who lived, reigned and passed away, without leaving any traces of history, except those numerous mounds containing a few bones and rude earthenware, to prove they ever existed.

February 23.—Nothing of importance.

February 24.—This has been a cold day. I am very unwell.

February 25.—I went to the hospital and received a dose of calomel. Another man was buried out of the third regiment, which makes two from that and three from this that lie mouldering in their mother earth at this encampment. We received orders to march close to town day after tomorrow, to be ready to embark.

February 26.—A fog rose from the lake just after daylight that obscured the rising sun, but before eight it fell in small drops leaving the sky clear. This night there is a great deal of fiddling and dancing, playing cards, drinking and making merry, in hopes of starting from here in the morning.

February 27.—We left the encampment without the hurry that usually has accompanied us and marched to town and came through it to the square; here we halted and rested. It is said the regiment made the best appearance of any regiment of volunteers in Tampico. We marched out of town on the northeast and crossed the bridge and encamped here among the other troops.

February 28.—The last of the winter, and every thing in market from soft corn to the tenderest ———. Mustered in.

March 1.—A light shower of rain last night. The troops have been shipping aboard vessels, and going to the mouth as fast as possible all day.

March 2.—Continued preparations to embark.

March 3.—I went out to the old Mexican fort,[29] that

[29] Fort Andonega.

stands on a point of the bluff one mile northwest from camp, and which formerly commanded the river from town to the mouth. It has once been a strong place, but now is in ruins, yet the roofless white walls make an imposing appearance at a distance. Just a few rods beyond the fort were some of the cavalry digging a grave for one of their companions, which is an easy job as the earth from nine or ten inches down consists of soft limestone. Leaving them, I went on back west until I came to a small Mexican arbor which had been built for lime. In this was a cavalryman, filling a haversack with lime. I asked him where to get water and he showed me a ditch in the bottom that led through the swamp to the pond north of town. Here in the swamp sunning themselves were several animals which look like coons but are more slender and have larger tails. On my approach they ran into a tree at the root. After drinking, I went back upon the highland and pursued my walk on the road that led back towards the interior. There is a thick growth of brush on each side of the road with an occasional banyan that rears its shady top far above the common growth like the mansion of some prince and his subjects. I turned in to one of these and found that there had been a house under it with a garden or park around: the house or shed was gone and nothing remains but the clear spot with the tree standing in the center. Up among the boughs was a platform made of sticks covered with palmetto and grass. The day being excessively hot I thought this an inviting place to rest, and the main trunk being leaning, roped with vinelike roots or small stems, I was soon stretched out in the shady top of a tree that overlooked the town, bay, river and encampments, while beneath was a yard several rods in circumference, with bushes around so thick that it appeared as if it were fenced in by a wall ten feet high, it was covered with flowering vines, among which were many pretty little singing birds. After reposing here a while I returned to camp.

March 4.—Warm and sunny. [Regiment] on dress parade.

March 5.—A large mail; I received a letter.

March 6.—Marched to town at twelve o'clock, ready to embark; lay in the Plaza all night without fire or any way to cook. At seven the band came to the flagstaff in the center of the square and played until nine o'clock.

March 7.—At eight o'clock we got into a small boat and rowed out to a small steamship which started to carry us over the bar. After running two hundred yards the boiler became injured so that she had to stop to repair; this took two hours. In the meantime the steamer *Orleans* passed us with three companies of this regiment aboard, also another steamboat that was ferrying some companies of our regiment to the ship. After mending the boiler, our vessel went on to the mouth, which is about six miles. There we saw the *Sheron of Bath*, our intended vessel, tossing her tall masts to and fro, with the steamboat lashed to her, while the men were passing in long boats from the steamer to the ship. We were soon over the bar amid the rolling billows, which tossed us from side to side. The ship attempted to fasten but missed, rounded and succeeded. Here commenced a scene hitherto unwitnessed by me, for the men were nearly all seasick, vomiting and heaving. No way to get aboard except by climbing up the side of the ship, which is a great deal higher than the boat, this all did without a single accident; the baggage was then drawn up by ropes. Then amid spewing, and seeking for bunks ended this day's scenes.

March 8.—Lay all day without unfurling the sails. We occupied our time in arranging our berths and suffering the processes of sea-sickness.

March 9.—Between three and four o'clock, a ship loaded with troops unfurled her sails and passed us. We gave them three cheers which she returned with waving caps and three swelling shouts that drowned the roar of the breakers. Our sailors quickly spread the canvass and then shot off to the eastward.

March 10.—The fore part of the day we sailed with a light breeze, and in the evening with a light gale in a southerly direction.

March 11.—A fair pleasant morning with a head wind which makes the skipper steer to the east. There are two or three vessels to be seen far ahead of us.

March 12.—Last night I was on guard and the sky was fair; the yards squared and the ship driving southward before a gentle stern wind, this increased to a gale, the dotted firmament was obscured by clouds. The gale drove our craft through the waves like a war horse with foam and fire flung around his breast. During the course of the night we passed several vessels, after daylight the wind subsided and the vessel rolled from side to side all day, still sailing southward.

March 13.—This is a warm day and we are sailing along the coast south of Vera Cruz. Late in the evening there came on a violent storm of wind and we put out to sea as fast as possible.

March 14.—A very blustery, stormy day.

March 15.—The wind blew almost as strong as yesterday. We are sailing about so as to creep as near to shore as possible. There is an occasional flock of flying fish to be seen, they seem to start up and sail off from one wave to the other.

March 16.—Our ship is still sailing amidst a heavy gale, and plowing amid the waves. Today we are lashing down our bunks, knocking up our heads amid our joy, revelry, song and merry-making to while away the tedious hours.

March 17.—The storm has sunk away to a modest breeze and we are sailing along the coast, against a head wind in sight of shore.

March 18.—Sailed all day with a fair wind, anchored at dark in the little harbor of [Sacrificios]. Here are forty-one or two transports. Just before we let loose the anchor, an officer came aboard from one of the ships and said that Taylor had fought and defeated Santa Anna near Saltillo,[30] that there had been some firing from the castle at our men that had killed several while at a battery. The men are in the best of spirits as if they were going to a ball.

March 19.—Set sail about ten o'clock and ran down among the shipping and anchored at dark; the castle has been firing all day.

March 20.—This morning the small boats came alongside the ship and we got ashore as fast as possible; this is three or four miles south of town. Here is the chief landing place of our army, and here are all the military stores. The town is surrounded from shore to shore which cuts off all communications with the interior. After forming on the beach, we marched out to our position in the line. This is about two miles from the landing, over black sand hills and hollows, overgrown with chaparral. We are stationed southwest of town on a narrow road that is scarcely wide enough for a wagon to pass.

March 21.—A false alarm last night. Some of us went back to the beach this morning to get provisions, and learned that the shipping had been injured a little by the storm last night, that a French vessel which ran the blockade and lay under the castle attempted to escape out to sea and was captured by the *Spitfire*, that both got aground on the reef while return-

[30] The First and Second Regiments of Illinois Infantry distinguished themselves in the Battle of Buena Vista.

Major General Robert Patterson, commander of Pennsylvania Volunteers, second in rank to Major General Winfield Scott. He is shown here after his service in the Civil War.

NATIONAL ARCHIVES

Landing of the American forces under General Scott south of Veracruz, March 9, 1847. There was virtually no opposition, and most of the troops were landed in a single day.

LIBRARY OF CONGRESS

The United States naval battery at the bombardment of Veracruz on March 22 and 23, 1847. The battery was composed of three heavy and four light guns from the squadron under Commodore Matthew C. Perry, who insisted that the naval officers accompany their guns.

LIBRARY OF CONGRESS

The bombardment of Veracruz, view from the sea.
LIBRARY OF CONGRESS

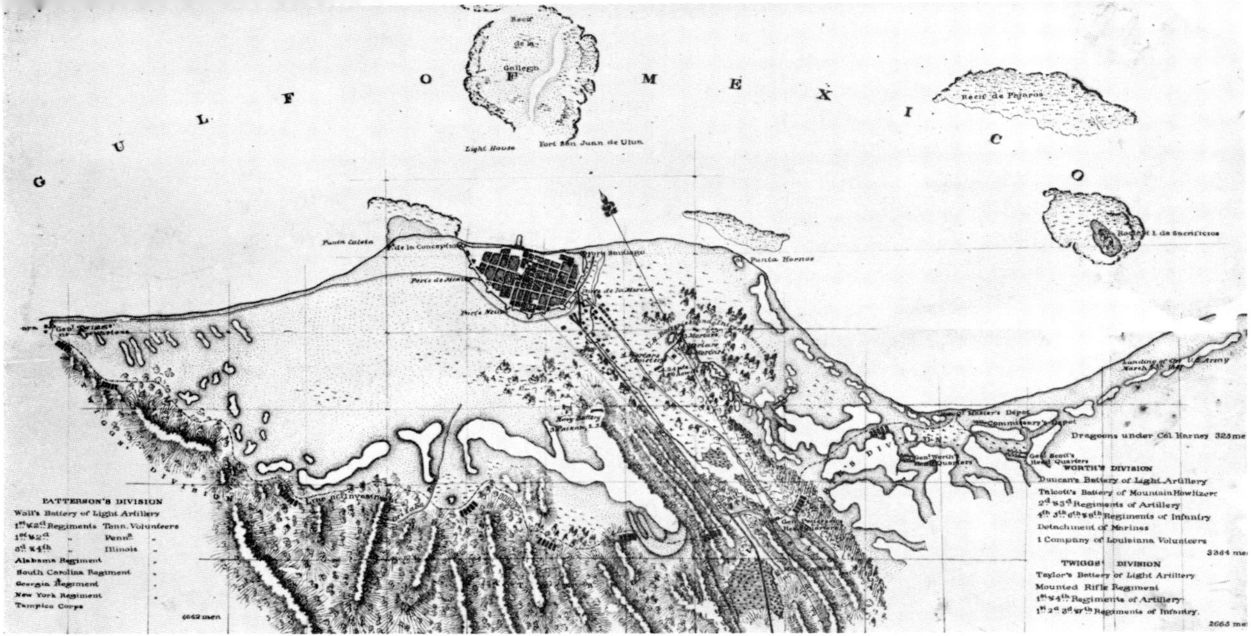

Map of the siege of Veracruz by United States troops under General Scott, March, 1847. Tennery's Fourth Illinois Regiment is listed with General Patterson's division, headquartered just right of the center of the map.

NATIONAL ARCHIVES

View of Cerro Gordo, showing Major General David E. Twiggs's division storming the main heights, April 18, 1847. Actually it was Brigadier General James Shields's brigade (commanded by Colonel Eward D. Baker) that made the main effort.

LIBRARY OF CONGRESS

The Battle of Cerro Gordo, April 18, 1847. Though credit for the victory was given to the regulars, it was the militia that did most of the fighting.

LIBRARY OF CONGRESS

Thomas D. Tennery and family about 1884. Seated: Sarah Alsop Tennery; Thomas D. Tennery; oldest child, Sarah Ann; and oldest son, John. Standing: younger children Julia Tennery Cook, Richard, Thomas, and Florie Estelle (called Fels). Another son, Samuel, had moved west, and Mary Jane, Samantha, Hannah, and George had died before the portrait was made.

ing. The enemy has been firing bombs and ball ever since we came, but without injury to us. The town appeared to be on fire twice today.

March 22.—Some of our men went out to kill beef today, they brought in some very good for this country. General Worth's[31] battery opened on the town this evening with bombs, and kept up the firing all night.[32]

March 23.—Captain Vinton[33] of the artillery was killed by a cannon ball last night. This regiment was ordered to march to Patterson's battery to work from four this evening to four in the morning. So we paraded, started and marched back as far as the railroad, which is half way to the beach; there we turned to the left and parallel with the railroad within five hundred yards of town. This battery has been erected without the enemy knowing it, being secured from their sight by chaparral bushes.

March 24.—At four o'clock this morning we left the battery, completed all except ——. Our first round is on the

[31] General William Jenkins Worth was born in New York in 1794. He served with distinction in the War of 1812, being severely wounded at Lundy's Lane. After the war he served as commandant of cadets and instructor in infantry tactics at West Point, 1820–28, though he was not a West Point graduate. He was promoted to colonel in 1838 and was breveted brigadier general in 1842 for his services as commander of army forces in the Seminole War. He served under Taylor in northern Mexico, and was breveted major general for his gallantry and meritorious service at Monterrey. Under Scott he won distinction at Veracruz, Cerro Gordo, and Churubusco. Worth was the first to enter Mexico City and received the surrender of the capital.

[32] Owing to rough weather no artillery had been landed before Tennery's arrival. After driving the Mexicans within the city walls, Worth's, Patterson's, and Pillow's troops surrounded the city from the south and relied on trenches to protect them from the Mexican artillery, which was answered only by American naval gunfire.

[33] Captain John Rogers Vinton entered the United States Military Academy in 1814 and from 1835 was a captain of the Third Artillery. He was breveted major for gallant conduct at Monterrey.

way a few minutes after daylight, the enemy opened on our battery which was doing great damage to their fortress. ———. Four of our men hit and killed at the guns, several wounded; there is a constant cannonading kept up day and night.[34]

March 25.—Still the cannons and bombs continue to roar. There was an order for our regiment to march out on the road about two miles west to engage some Mexicans, who were reported to be there. We started at four P.M., marched about four miles and met some men fetching in some beef. They said they had seen a number of [Mexican] cavalry and went back to show us the place. When we got there no enemy was to be seen. Some went to hunt beef, and the rest started back to camp, where we arrived a good deal after dark. Those that went to hunt beef came in a little while afterwards, and stated that they saw a few men on a hill, whom they supposed to be Mexicans. As we went out, there was some sharp firing off to the left which is said to have been an engagement between the dragoons and the enemy. Near eleven, there was an alarm caused by firing toward town.

March 26.—Last night when we came back to camp, the cannon had ceased their roar, on account of a truce, but commenced about one this morning and continued until six. The enemy did not return the fire, but again asked for a truce which is still continued.

March 27.—The night has passed without any noise or disturbance; everything is still and quiet which makes us feel a degree of cheerfulness that none with a pure heart

[34] This battery, also called the Naval Battery or Battery No. 5, mounted three 68-pounders and three 32-pounders. Patterson's men managed to install all but one of the guns under cover of darkness. The last one was rashly moved in during daylight, but without being detected by the Mexicans.

could experience while the work of death was going on; the day has passed over with quietude. The town has surrendered.

March 28.—There was a light sprinkle of rain last night. We understood the town has surrendered on condition that we take possession of the town and castle with all of the artillery, arms and public stores, and that we are to hold the same until redeemed by the Mexican government. The prisoners [are] to be let go on condition that they shall serve no more in the present war, unless exchanged or released by our government from the present engagement. This has been a clear still day but cool. A flock or two of brants passed over to the northward this morning.

March 29.—The Mexican army marched out of town and stacked their arms in the presence of our army. This was at nine o'clock A.M. It was truly a solemn scene. They passed through the south gate and stacked their arms on the plain near the railroad, about half a mile from town. Our troops took position and hoisted the Stars and Stripes over the town and the castle.

March 30.—Several of the boys have been to town; they have brought out some scopets[35] and old swords, which I suppose they intend shall be great trophies when they get home.

March 31.—We left our position in the chaparral, and marched across close to the battery. We are encamped between the cemetery, and back of a beautiful green level surrounded by sand hills.

April 1.—Finished moving our baggage. Lieutenant Wheat,[36] of the Tennessee cavalry, is raising a company of

[35] Escopetas, Mexican weapons similar to carbines.
[36] Captain Chatham R. Wheat, Tennessee Mounted Volunteers.

cavalry for [service] during the war. Several of this company have joined; today they elected their officers.

April 2.—We have heard this evening that General Quitman, on his way to Alvarado, met some of the enemy's forces on the twenty-first and defeated them.

April 3.—It is reported that Colonel Harney's[37] men have taken two [Mexican] lieutenants and thirteen privates, somewhere near here today.

April 4.—Clear, warm, calm day.

April 5.—At dress parade, orders were read that on our march to the interior, we should reduce our baggage to the least possible amount. A great deal of thundering and lightning in the west after nightfall.

April 6.—I went to the city today. It is a close solid built place, but appears very old and exhibits signs of former greatness. At this time it is on the decline. The church on the Plaza is a very large, venerable, old, time-stained, storm-beaten building, but the interior has a clean, neat appearance and is well stored with images and artificial flowers. The walls of the city are built chiefly of coral and brick, cemented with lime. In passing through this place an unaccountable feeling will steal almost over one, and his mind is taken back to the days of the Montezuma, the landing of Cortez, his conquests and overthrow of the government, the long tyrannical reign of the Spaniards, the cruelty displayed by those professing Christians, and finally the revolution and liberation of the country. Also the distracted government afterwards, which can never be otherwise while connected with their religion and a prey to priestcraft. At every

[37] Colonel William S. Harney, Scott's cavalry commander, was commissioned second lieutenant in 1818 and by 1846 had been promoted to colonel, having been breveted colonel in 1840 for gallantry in the Seminole War. On April 18, 1847, he was breveted brigadier general for gallantry at Cerro Gordo.

turn and angle as posts, these seem to tell a tale of woe and misery for upwards of three hundred years. The mind is brought down to the present time and inevitably inquires what shall be the result of the present war, or who and how shall it be governed when ended. But it is vain to try to look into the book of fate until the leaves are turned. The streets are filthy and have a bad smell, the town presents a mass of old partly ruined buildings with heaps of rubbish here and there knocked down by the recent bombardment. Add to this the wall of the city with its many forts and batteries still mounted with guns and mortars and it makes quite an interesting place.

April 7.—On parade this evening, orders were read that we should march on the ninth.

April 8.—Moved all the extra baggage to town to be stored until we return.

April 9.—We loaded up the baggage and paraded, then stacked arms until our brigade passed, then took arms and marched to the walls of the city and turned around close to the railroad depot, where we stopped for two hours until all the baggage wagons passed, then started and left the city, marching west with the beach to the right of the gulf; here we halted and stacked arms and our company was ordered to stay as guards to protect a train of wagons that was to come out of the city. This detained us until four; then we started but got on very slow on account of the wagons being overloaded. At night we stopped and lay with the wagons.

April 10.—The train geared up and tried to start, but found they could not get along, then unloaded and went back to town to try for stronger teams. We stayed to guard the stuff. About nine a team came up and stated that the same teams were coming back again.

April 11.—The wagons came early as usual and commenced loading, but an order came for us to go on and join the regiment. Accordingly we started and after marching about three miles came to a prairie with plenty of horned cattle grazing on it. After marching seven or eight miles we came to a ranch; near it we saw a dead soldier, laying under some bushes by the side of the road. There are soldiers straggling which shows bad discipline in their corps. There are splendid culverts and bridges on this road. After travelling eighteen miles we camped at a bridge with Cos. B, C, and G, and also the train; it had overtaken us.

April 12.—Left the camp at four o'clock and marched twelve miles over a rough country and stopped at a bridge over a small river that runs a northeast course toward the gulf. The bridge is one of the grandest pieces of masonry, being built of stone and plastered with lime cement. The arches are large and high, supported on strong pillars. Upon a point that overlooks the whole country is a small fort; it is one of the strongest positions in the world but abandoned at this time. On this side is a small barracks and some fine houses, one especially, near the top of the hill, very fine compared with anything we have seen in this country.[38] We left this place at three o'clock, and marched thirteen miles mostly over a level country and came to camp. It is in a bottom between two small streams.

April 13.—We learned that yesterday when the front guard came here they had a skirmish with some of the enemy, but soon made them vanish. General Twiggs' division went on a few miles and found the enemy had fortified positions in some hills that commanded the road, so after exchanging a few shots they came back to wait until all the brigades came up. This day has passed off without anything

[38] One of three haciendas belonging to General Santa Anna, all located on the National Highway.

of importance occurring. By going up on a high hill close to this place, we can see the flag and fortifications of the enemy, our whole army spread out in this peaceful valley, the three gorgeous bridges over as many mountain streams that come leaping from rock to rock and unite a little ways below on their way to the gulf, which can still be seen in the distance.

April 14.—This morning two or three of the third regiment went to a watering place a mile or so above here and found some Mexican soldiers at a ranch. They all escaped but one whom they took prisoner. He was armed with a sword and in uniform. Today we were down below here about a mile to a spring and small dripping cave, the water pours down from the rocks twenty or thirty feet high. There are a great many spars or stone substances like icicles formed by water, suspended from the upper part of the cave, some of which extend to the bottom. It has the appearance of water falling from a precipice and freezing, but the spars are not transparent and look dark like stained limestone. General Scott came up this evening with a company of dragoons from Vera Cruz.

April 15.—General Shields, Colonel Baker and Major Harris with twenty of us went out this morning to reconnoitre the position of the enemy; so we went up on a ridge that runs parallel to the one they occupy, and about seven or eight hundred yards from it, where we could see the line and breast works of the enemy, and a small fort on a high hill. We could see the soldiers all about the hill and at work. They fired a few guns at us but without injury, and our men fired three guns at some of them down in a hollow. Afterwards they fired a cannon at us; this made us more cautious. Then we went farther and saw a body of cavalry far to the left. When we came back we learned that Captain Jones of Co. C had been out with a party of men, that a few

Mexicans had surprised them, so that they left the captain who was trying to halt his men. Then he fell in with four or five of Co. H. They fired on the advancing enemy, one in the act of aiming at the captain, this made them vanish. A little blood was found on the ground occupied by the Mexicans but no men. After we came in two men were trying to draw the load from a gun, when it fired. The load went through the breast of the one that held the ramrod, while the rod went through the neck and lodged in it, of a man passing behind him. Mack Rees, the one that was shot through the breast died almost instantly, but Williams, the one wounded in the neck, is still alive. There is thunder and lightning and rain this evening from the west.

April 16.—One of the second regiment of Tennessee volunteers was out in the woods this morning and got shot through the foot, whether by accident or the enemy we cannot tell. Also some of the same regiment went about four miles down the stream to hunt beef. Two or three left the rest; afterwards the main body heard the report of guns and went to the place and found one of their comrades wounded with seven balls. He was past speaking; his gun and cartridge box were gone. They brought him in but he died soon afterwards. An escort went out with the butchers about seven miles, where they killed several wagon loads of beef. Here they had a skirmish and two of the cavalry were wounded, one in the foot, the other in the thigh. Several men came up this evening from the bridge thirteen miles back, where Worth lay last night.

April 17.—Twiggs' brigade started out toward the line of the enemy at day break. About ten or eleven we heard the firing of cannon and musketry; directly we received orders to fill our canteens and have haversacks ready to move at a moment's warning. As soon as we were ready, we started out along the National road, occasionally meeting some of the boys with prisoners, or a soldier with a bleeding arm or hand. After marching about four miles we turned off the road to the right, along a new cut way. Here we passed about two hundred men drawing a large gun across a hollow. From this on we kept passing men until we got where the wounded men were. This was a shocking sight to see, men mangled in every form, some with their limbs amputated. The cannon balls were whistling over our heads occasionally. We stopped at the side of a hill which the riflemen had taken. This was the battle of today. The Mexican boys were great but they retired in good order. After dark we succeeded in getting the large gun on top of the hill and two or three small ones.

April 18.—Just at daylight this morning, some of the boys came out from Plan del Rio, with breakfast which they had been sent back for. We learned from them that a party hunting yesterday was attacked at a spring and Moses Shelton, of Co. D, was killed, one more was wounded. The grape soon began to fall among us but without injury. The order was to fall in, so we started, the third regiment in front, ours next, the New York in the rear. Our path lay along the hollow and was soon exposed to the view of the enemy on the high hill, which caused cannon shot to roar above our heads and batter the rocks in the hollow to our right. After travelling this way a while, we were ordered to file right and move up the opposite steep at double quick, here Lieutenant Cowden fell and orderly Hanchy was wounded.[39] The grape rattled like hail when we gained the level ground; we bore to the left along a narrow path at double quick in single file. In passing along this path we saw a splendid

[39] First Lieutenant George W. Cowardan and First Sergeant John M. Handchey, both of Company I, Fourth Illinois Infantry.

scene, the infantry under Twiggs was charging the hill; the steepness rendered the progress slow, but they moved on steady, firing and loading at will, with a firmness that never can be excelled, while red flame seemed constantly to blaze along the lines of the enemy, which were supported by their cannon. A burst of admiration broke from our troop in three cheers that for a moment stunned the roar of the battle. At this time the front companies of our regiment came in view of the batteries, by the path opening into the field, we got before (*i.e.*, in front) when we ran up the hill. Here the batteries opened up on us. We flanked to the right, and fell on the enemy at some ranches where they had their military stores and hospitals. This is on the road. Here we had all kinds of fighting; Lieutenant [Richard] Murphy, Private [Joshua E.] Jackson, [Leroy] Thornby and myself were wounded of our company, Jackson in the head, Lieut. in the lower part of the body, both mortal, Thornby just over the hip, myself through both legs. A part of our regiment and a part of the Yorkers, Twiggs and the cavalry charged (pursued) them within four miles of Jalapa. General Pillow's brigade had attacked in front, Twiggs on the left and Shields in the rear of the enemy. Twiggs and Shields succeeded in routing the enemy. Pillow's division was driven back in the first attempt to charge, but General [R. Díaz de] La Vega, seeing all was lost, and that he would soon be attacked in the rear, surrendered to him. Where Pillow's men attacked it was impossible ever to make a successful charge. This place is called Cerro Gordo. When I was wounded I called Perryman who took care of [me] the balance of the day.

April 19.—I lay last night at a ranch, where a great many of the wounded had been taken, among the rest Thornby and Jackson. The lieutenant was carried down to Plan del

Rio last night. The army is constantly going by. The prisoners taken yesterday were turned loose today and went to Jalapa unarmed. La Vega escaped; he would not take the oath to serve no more during the present war. Those of our company that were here went on except [Sergeant Absolom] Hamilton and [Corporal Isaiah] Davenport, left to attend the sick.

April 20.—Jackson appears quite peart today, we all think we are mending. The Mexican hospital is across the way from us and they keep up a groaning. Our men are moving the baggage and stores of provisions captured from this place to Jalapa.

April 21.—A man died this morning, and Lieutenant Murphy at Plan del Rio. Joshua E. Jackson died about eleven o'clock.

April 22.—The men are destroying the Mexican magazines and collecting their scattered arms and breaking them up.

April 23.—Men are passing to and fro all the time, a great many on their way to Jalapa. Mexicans poking about, and buzzards floating over the battle field or preying on the carcasses of the dead. Some Mexicans passed here today with fat hogs, driving them to Vera Cruz. They gave the cook a very fine one for us.

April 24.—The Mexicans have been passing along towards Vera Cruz today with pack mules and some cars carried between mules. Our troops furnished wagons and the Mexicans have moved their wounded to Jalapa.

April 25.—A train came from Jalapa to move us. There was one of the Tennessee troops burned his hand very badly today. It was only yesterday he burned the other one; now I suppose he will quit playing with fire and powder, at least until his hands get well.

April 26.—Breakfast over this morning, we were loaded into wagons and started. The road being paved, we were jostled almost to death. The greater part of the way the road is a gentle ascent; on each side is various scenery, sometime plains, then ranges of hills or an isolated cone that appears like some stupendous rock thrown by nature in sportive play to mock the puny art of man. On each side are green bushes, many of which are in bloom. Within about eight miles of Jalapa we passed Santa Anna's hacienda or farm house; this is off the road to the left. From there we occasionally passed a ranch, with patches of bananas, also peach trees with peaches on them as large as quail eggs, besides fruit of various other kinds. Along the road are some good stone fences. We got to Jalapa about sundown, and are quartered upstairs in a room connected with a church.

April 27.—Awoke this morning after laying on our hard pads and suffering with our irritated wounds, and annoyed by the bells of the city. This is a cool cloudy day. The rest of the wounded came in this evening. Many of them had to be carried in litters; this was very fatiguing to the men. We learned from the men that a regular, helping to carry a litter, swore last night when they stopped, that before he would carry another day, he would kill himself; so this morning about an hour before they got ready to start, he loaded his gun, took off his shoes and socks, lent on the muzzle of the gun, pulled the trigger with his big toe and blew the load through him. Despondency ended his life.

April 28.—[Private Joseph] Thorp of Co. G died this morning, the second one of the company who has died from the battle. Captain Newcom came up yesterday with Seargs. [William] Lowry, [John Vinson] Vincent and Pratt Sawyer, who had been left at Point Isabel. Men are dying in the hospital almost constantly. We moved out of the small room that we occupied, and got into a large spacious one on the ground floor, the windows look out on part of the town and the hills beyond. There was a shower of rain today; these thunder showers occur almost every day. William Clifton came up. Uriah Davenport of Co. I is expected to die of lockjaw. He was wounded in the foot but did not attend to it, and stayed at the camp until yesterday.

April 30.—Sergeant Davenport of Co. I died. Some of the third regiment went out yesterday. They were attacked and lay out all night. One of them was killed this morning, two or three companies went out and had a skirmish; they killed two Mexican soldiers. One of the New Yorkers was brought in this evening but almost done [beaten] to death, supposed to be done by some soldiers or bad men belonging to the army.

May 1.—Sergeant Allen of Co. E of this regiment died last night. His thigh was broken in the battle of Cerro Gordo on the eighteenth of April.

May 2.—General Patterson visited the hospital today, and enquired after our condition.

May 3.—A great many of the third and fourth regiment boys have obtained furloughs and have hired to the quartermaster to drive mules to Vera Cruz, or wagons as the case may be. They engage until the sixth of June. Some of them started yesterday for Vera Cruz.[40] Lieutenant Moby[41] started home.

May 4.—[Private Henry] Billsboro of Co. G was brought in this evening, beaten almost to death. He left with the

[40] The actual period of enlistment for the regiment was April 30, 1846, to May 29, 1847.

[41] Second Lieutenant Charles Maltby, Company E, Fourth Illinois Infantry. He was wounded at Cerro Gordo.

train that started yesterday, got behind, two Mexicans attacked him, he snapped his gun at one of them. They fell to work and would have killed him had it not been for some dragoons that came up.

May 5.—Depau [Private James Depew] of Co. B, got a wound in his left arm, but [doctors] could not find what went with the bullet until this morning, when it came out of the same hole it went in. They say one regiment is to start home tomorrow, and Major Harris[42] was inquiring who would be able to go along with them.

May 6.—This is the day fixed upon for our troops to start home; the whole fore-part of the day is spent in visiting us and preparing to go, for the greater part of our wounded is to go with the regiment. At length the parting moment arrived. We bid farewell with mingled emotions, after having been with them nearly a year, and knowing that they were about to return to their friends which calls up our warmest emotions, and kindles the desire to go with them. There is five of our company left at this place, Lowry, Thornby, and myself, also [Corporal] William Kenney to tend us. There are but five or six others of the regiment left.

May 7.—This morning I can walk around the room a little and look out of the windows to the south which opens on a part of the city occupied by pleasant gardens, filled with almost every variety of vegetables and fruits, with pools of clear water, with here and there a fine house presenting an appearance of comfort and ease seldom to be met with. Still beyond them are fields of barley, maize, etc., until the hills rise up in bold relief, extending to the mountains which terminate where Orizaba rises to the very distant clouds and is often seen above them. This peak is northwest of this place

[42] Major Thomas L. Harris, third-ranking officer of the Fourth Illinois Infantry.

distant about thirty miles, and rises in a cone-like shape. Its top, and a good ways down from its summit, is covered with eternal snow, which gives it a sublime and picturesque appearance. The high mountains still extend to the west but not quite so high.

May 8.—The hospital was inspected by Dr. Bite[43] and some other physicians.

May 9.—Yesterday and today are long to be remembered as the era [anniversary] when open hostilities between Mexico and our government began.

May 10.—The boys brought in some cherries and gave me some; they are of the black kind and taste the same as in the states. A few of the regulars brought in a soldier not able to speak or help himself, besides they had let him get so nasty he was covered with fly blows. Here they left him without any attendance, such meanness is often seen among the regulars.

May 11.—A man died in this room today.

May 12.—General Scott visited the hospital, familiarly enquiring of each patient concerning his health, disease and to what corps he belonged and so forth.

May 13.—Lieutenant Janson[44] died last night. His sufferings were great. There has been no rain since the sixth of this month.

May 14.—There is a large train of wagons coming from Vera Cruz. One man died in the ward this evening; four or five die every day in the hospital.

May 15.—Nothing more than usual. Nine or ten are buried and as fast as they are taken out others are brought in.

May 16.—As it is Sunday, there is a very full market. Cap-

[43] Not identified.

[44] Second Lieutenant Sheldon J. Johnson, Company F, Fourth Illinois Infantry.

tain Mason[45] of the rifle regiment was buried this evening. He was buried at the English graveyard a quarter of a mile south of this place. The funeral procession was a fine and solemn one.

May 17.—The singing birds hail the dawn of day with their warbling choir, the rising sun gilds the east with a flood of golden light, and the dark mountains reared up in the west, their figures glittering with snow make a grand and pleasing appearance. About one o'clock there was thunder and a pattering of rain; afterward there was plenty of snow to be seen on the mountains west of here.

May 18.—A beautiful clear day until evening; then the west became cloudy, the thunder rolled through the skies. The foggy clouds gathered on the mountains and had the whitish appearance of snow clouds in our northern winters. The stormy wind and clouds played over us in fitful gusts, while the fresh, pleasant cool air passed through the streets.

May 19.—Fair morning and cloudy evening as usual. Five soldiers were tied up and whipped this evening in public market. No doubt they were guilty of the crime alleged against them and received their just deserts. But still it chills one's blood to see free born Americans tied up and whipped like dogs, in a market yard in a foreign land.

May 20.—At one o'clock this evening a South Carolina volunteer died in this room. We have had a hard rain, the first since the sixth.

May 21.—Several deaths but nothing more than usual. Cloudy but no rain.

May 22.—There is talk of a train starting to Vera Cruz in a few days. We are in a peck of trouble [worried] for fear we will not get to go with it. A hard shower this evening.

[45] Captain Stevens T. Mason, of a mounted rifle company of the Regular Army. He died on May 15, 1847, of wounds received at Cerro Gordo.

May 23.—Sunday. The market is crowded with all kinds of vegetables. The day has passed off without rain.

May 24.—We reported ourselves to Captain Whiting[46] for conveyance to Vera Cruz. There is a company of cavalry arrived here this evening from Vera Cruz. We expect to leave this place Wednesday.

May 25.—Nothing of importance. A great many expecting to go away tomorrow. Just after dark, there was a splendid procession of the priests with burning candles in their hands, to be seen in the streets escorted by our officers and soldiers.

May 26.—A great many disappointed as to starting home, I among the rest. After a wagon being sent and us getting in we had to unload and stay. Cass[47] started without any of the fourth regiment except Kenney of our Co. and Jenkins of Co. B who were both able to take care of themselves. There are about one hundred discharged men starting home with seven or eight wagons.

May 27.—I have had a walk today out to the cotton factory; it is about a quarter of a mile from here. It is owned by an Englishman and worked by water power. The stream is a small branch in a deep ravine that commences at the road that goes out toward Orizaba, here where the road crosses, the water falls about thirty feet, then the pond extends to the dam. It is about thirty feet high, built of stone cemented together with waterproof lime. This is a splendid work; the factory buildings are connected with it, and built of the same material. From the factory we can see the whole town,

[46] Captain Daniel Powers Whiting, a regular, who was shortly thereafter breveted major for gallantry and meritorious conduct at Cerro Gordo.

[47] Perhaps Dr. Alexander M. Cassidy, or possibly Private Archibald Cast of Company D, the wardmaster in the hospital at Jalapa. Both Corporal Kinney and Private James M. Jenkins had been attendants there.

as it is built on a site inclined to the south, and a high hill which is north, and the mountains west, with many ranches and farms on its side, among its elevated valleys. The scene is one of nature's grandest.

May 28.—The street that runs west from the gate of this monastery leads out towards the mountains, goes past the slaughter house at the farther edge of town. There is an old ruined church out here, the yard of which is used by us as a graveyard. I witnessed the burial of three men there today, all in one grave. There is coffee growing here in the gardens, it grows on a small shrub, which looks very much like the black haw, from eight to ten feet high: the berry contains two grains, and grows on the twigs like clusters of plums.

May 29.—How it is I cannot say, but as sure as one is confined to a room after being sick or wounded, so sure they will spend sleepless nights. This is the case of many of us. Last night I got up and went out in the yard. The moon shone bright; all was still except the sentinel, the silent measured tread of his moving shadow still showed that he was on duty. The police or city watch would occasionally pass along in the shade of the houses. But all else was still, not a dog moved his tongue, every leaf was at rest, the dark mountains in the west shone like a threatening cloud whose desire it was to wrap this city of reposing beauty in stormy darkness, yet strange as it may appear, the snowy peaks of Orizaba showed in the distance like a beam of light, a star of hope on a tower of nature's own erection, completing the grandeur of the night scenery. Nothing of importance today.

May 30.—The market yard is full of all kinds of vegetables. A great many of the marketeers are Indians or full-blood aborigines, they wear coarse woolen garments of a bluish color. All the produce is packed in, and often the natives are to be seen with a sack on their backs containing a child, besides the produce designed for market. They carry the load by a strap across the head fastened to the load.

May 31.—Cool, pleasant and airy. Thornby[48] died at 9:50 P.M. He had borne his illness with a fortitude and patience, worthy of the most exalted praise and exhibited in his disposition a noble character. In all his sickness he has never complained or fretted, but submitted to fate with the most sublime fortitude.

June 1.—Cool and rain in the afternoon.

June 2.—[Private] William Morris of Co. K died last night. He was wounded in the battle of Cerro Gordo, and had his leg amputated, but after his wounds had healed, he took the fever and died after suffering so much.

June 3.—As this is Corpus Christi Day, there are a great many in church. The market is over-crowded, there is a great deal of talk among the soldiers [and] among the rest that this town is in imminent danger of recapture by Mexican robbers or rather liars.

June 4.—I was down at the washing place. It is where the stream runs through under the bridge and falls at the head of the factory pond. This contrivance is the greatest for washing I ever saw, the water runs through a pipe of cement; on each side of this are square holes eighteen inches apart and the same in width. These holes are full of water; the spaces are inclined alike, and are used as washboards. Along the sides of the pipes are gutters that run off the suds and so forth. This is covered and built of stone and cement. There are to be seen nearly a hundred women at all times of the day washing, which they do the best and fastest I ever saw. They spread the white garments on the grass in the sunshine, and throw water on them until they are white to perfection.

48 Private Leroy Thornby, Company E, Fourth Illinois Infantry.

Besides this there are other washing places in town of the same construction.

June 5.—A man by the name of Plunkett died in this room today.[49] He belonged to the second regiment of Tennessee volunteers, and had his arm amputated because of a wound, but it got well though he suffered a great deal from other causes.

June 6.—Sabbath. I went to church. This is a splendid edifice. The people are on their knees the greater part of the time during services. There are but a few seats in the church; the congregation worship standing or kneeling. The church is grand and finely ornamented inside. In time of service, they keep more than one hundred candles burning. A great deal of talk about a train starting home or to Vera Cruz.

June 7.—A train came from Perote. A wagon load [of dead men] was hauled to the grave; this occurs every day. Plunkett among the rest.

June 8.—We started home at two o'clock P.M. after great exertion on Captain Davis'[50] part to get wagons for us. We had to leave Todd.[51] There are eleven of us Illinois boys, of the fourth regiment along and one of the third. We came out about eight miles and lay at an old deserted building. There are about one hundred and forty of us. No language can describe our feelings on this occasion. We are starting home after being twelve months absent. I am just out of a hospital, where we have been confined six weeks, and every day witnessed the death of one or more of our countrymen and we have to leave behind some of our dearest friends.

49 Private B. Plunkett, Company E, Second Tennessee Volunteers.

50 Captain Charles W. Davis, a regular, assistant quartermaster for volunteers.

51 Private James I. D. Todd, Fourth Illinois Infantry, appears on the roster of Company I with the note, "Left wounded in hospital at Jalapa, May 7, 1847."

Coming out of the hospital all looks green and fresh, the pleasant air peculiar to this country fans us. We are leaving the tall mountains behind. Before us is a descending plane, dipping toward the gulf, all covered with everlasting green, except where Orizaba rears its snow white top toward the heavens, while clouds with gilded edges streak its breast.

June 10.—We awoke this morning just before day, by an alarm raised on account of the discovery of some brush placed on the bridge, its object evidently to bother the teams. We moved up to the barracks, and waited until day. Then we could discover nothing of the enemy, so we threw the brush out of the way and started across. While on the bridge the enemy made its appearance on the right bluff and commenced a brisk fire with escopettes and muskets, which killed two men, a wagon master and one more. Sergeant Lowry[52] was crossing the bridge at the time; he stopped with two others and returned their fire. He tumbled one down the precipice, then six lancers came on the other end of the bridge; he shot twice and brought one of them down. In the meantime we got up the hill on this side as fast as possible, when they contented themselves by watching us on their horses. We moved on to the ranch this side (expecting an attack every moment). Here we found about one thousand of General Cadwalader's[53] men. They informed us that they left Vera Cruz, four days since, that they had four skirmishes and lost several men and about thirty wagons on

[52] Sergeant William Lowry, Company E, Fourth Infantry.

[53] General George Cadwalader, brigadier general of Pennsylvania Volunteers, won a commendation for the action described in this and subsequent entries. He later won a brevet promotion to major general for his gallant and meritorious conduct in the Battle of Chapultepec, and was released from active duty on July 20, 1848. On April 19, 1861, he again entered active duty as major general of Pennsylvania Volunteers and served until July 5, 1865. He died on February 3, 1879.

the way; most of the fighting had been in the vicinity of the next bridge. They had sent back for some field pieces. Just at night six hundred came up with some mountain howitzers; they had seen a body of cavalry at some distance from the road.

June 11.—A thunder shower in the fore part of last night. We can see the Mexicans on the hills in every direction this morning. Near eleven o'clock they commenced firing from the hills in front. Their balls fell among our men without injury; a few of our men went up and ran them off. We started at eight and came on to the next bridge, six miles, and watered. For miles on each side of this are broken wagons, thrown away provisions, etc. About sundown we met some cavalry. We travelled until about ten and got here to the long bridge. Here are two companies going up with some wagons.

June 12.—Started in the morning and came to Santa Fe, halted a few minutes and came to Vera Cruz, and got aboard the steamer *Galveston.*

June 14.—Lay still all day, loading on coal to burn in crossing. Have drawn no provisions yet.

June 15.—A thunder shower last night. It is reported that General Cadwalader's men were attacked in crossing the National bridge on the evening of the eleventh, and lost some thirty in killed and wounded. We finished loading coal, and started at four P.M. How rejoiced the heart at leaving this country, where we have endured hardships, been exposed in battles, been in hospitals, and seen death, misery and suffering in every shape and form. Suffered from tyranny practiced, had the right of American soldiers trampled on by their own officers. Besides we are leaving a sickly country to return to our own peaceful homes. Yet we have the dangers of the sea to pass. The setting sun throws back a flood of orange light as he sinks behind the tall Cordilleras, which appears to rise out of the deep blue sea far to the west. Around us all is still and calm except the current of air produced by the motion of the boat, while her black smoke from the funnels, points like a finger of scorn at Vera Cruz in the rear, that city of woe and misery.

June 16.—Calm day, nothing doing, blue sea, sailing lively.

June 17.—Cloudy and stormy. The rolls and swells tossing the boat from side to side. Occasionally a beautiful flying fish will rise from a wave and skim over the water like a swallow, now dipping, then up again, then into its native element and seen no more.

June 18.—Fair day but rough sea.

June 19.—Fair morning. There are many smooth places, or roads, left on the water by passing craft. We keep a sharp lookout for land, but can only see a few sail. About ten o'clock we met the ship *John Garrow* bound for Liverpool, that came out of New Orleans on Wednesday and reckoned it one hundred miles from the mouth of the river; we entered it and now are running up it.

June 20.—When I awoke, we were sailing up past the lower part of New Orleans. We landed in Lafayette. Took lodgings at Mrs. Bell's near engine [Company] No. 2.

June 22.—Went to the paymaster's office at commercial exchange; part of us received pay. The second Ohio regiment is here, and one regiment of Missouri Cavalry.[54] I saw Captain Julien[55] of the Ohio regiment, paying as [fast as] possible. Got our pay, went aboard the steamer *Hancock*, sailed

[54] Colonel Doniphan's famous regiment, on its way home after the epic march through Chihuahua. See page *xxiii* of the Introduction.

[55] Captain Evan Julian, Second Ohio Infantry.

at six P.M. All the boats are crowded with troops returning home.

June 23.—Riding on the river with constantly changing scene, passing boats, etc. Passed Baton Rouge today.

June 24.—Passed Vicksburg racing with the *Whiteville.* Rain at eleven o'clock.

June 25.—*Huntsville* passed us; a hard rain.

June 26.—Passed Memphis.

June 27.—Near three o'clock P.M. we arrived at Cairo, Ill.

June 28.—At one, landed at St. Louis and stopped at the Virginia house.

June 29.—Got into a market wagon and crossed over onto Illinois, put up at —— house, —— came out about thirty miles.

June 30.—Got to Salem.

July 1.—Hired a young man to take me home.

EPILOGUE

Epilogue

UPON reaching his home in Illinois, Thomas Tennery resumed the quiet life he had interrupted a year earlier. He purchased an additional forty acres of land, this time paying $2.50 an acre, and spent several years improving it. On February 7, 1850, he married Sarah E. Allsop, the daughter of a neighboring family recently arrived from England. In 1851, Tennery and his wife moved to his original farm, and in 1853 to a new farm they had purchased nearby. There they reared their family and made their home until their deaths in the early 1890's.

Tennery served his township in various ways. He was a supervisor for several terms and a justice of the peace. He built one of the first churches in the community, and the first schoolhouse, in which he served as the first teacher. He continued to farm, although he had been somewhat disabled by his leg wounds. The records of the Veterans Administration show that he received a pension of eight dollars a month until his death in 1891 and that his widow claimed the pension thereafter for the short period that she outlived him.

Among Tennery's fellow veterans of the Fourth Illinois Regiment, Major Thomas Langrell Harris, a Connecticut-born graduate of Trinity College who had studied law and had been admitted to the bar in 1842, had been elected county school commissioner in Illinois in 1845. He raised one company of the Fourth Illinois Volunteers, of which he was captain and later regimental major. In 1846 he was elected *in absentia* to the Illinois legislature. Upon his return to Illinois, he was voted a sword by the state for gallantry at the Battle of Cerro Gordo and was later elected to the United State House of Representatives. He served in Congress from 1849 to 1851 and from 1855 to 1858, when he died at the age of forty-two.

The regimental commander, Colonel Edward D. Baker, was a member of Congress when the Mexican War began. He returned to civilian life with the members of his regiment, and in 1848 was re-elected to the House of Representatives, but was disappointed that Taylor did not offer him a cabinet post. In 1851, after one term in the House, Baker obtained a grading contract for the Panama Railway. In 1852 he moved to California, where he quickly gained prominence as a lawyer and public speaker. A Whig, and later a Republican, Baker belonged to the minority party, and he did not improve his political prospects when he defended the murderer Cora against the vigilantes in San Francisco in 1856. He continued to be highly regarded as an orator, however, and was selected to speak at the funeral of Senator David C. Broderick in 1859. Some months thereafter he was invited to Oregon, where he was assured the Republican nomination to the United States Senate. In October, 1860, he was elected by a combination of Republicans and Douglas Democrats in opposition to the incumbent, General Joseph Lane, another Mexican War hero, who had also served as Oregon's first territorial governor and delegate to Congress.

On his way east, Baker stopped in San Francisco and spoke at a large testimonial gathering in his honor. It is possible that the plea he made for the Union may have helped Lincoln carry California in the election a few days later. In any case, as the only Republican senator from the West Coast, and as an old friend of Lincoln, Baker was invited to Springfield in December, 1860, for consultations about secessionist activities in the Pacific states. During the ensuing months he delivered many famous and effective speeches on behalf of the Union. In April, 1861, he again raised a regiment, which was called the California Regiment though enlisted in New York and Pennsylvania. Eventually enlistments raised the regiment to brigade size, and he was offered a commission as a brigadier and later as a major general. Baker declined both offers, since to accept would have meant that he must resign his seat in the Senate. He was killed at the Battle of Ball's Bluff in October, 1861.

Brigadier General James Shields, who commanded the Brigade of Illinois Volunteers, of which the Fourth Regiment was a part, had a career closely resembling Baker's. Shields had also settled in Illinois, read and practiced law and engaged in politics, fought in the Black Hawk War, and served in the state legislature. Though he was himself a Democrat, he and Lincoln became good friends. He was shot through the chest at Cerro Gordo, but miraculously recovered and was breveted major general. He led a brigade at the Battle of Churubusco. When the war ended, he returned to Illinois. Appointed territorial governor of Oregon, he resigned the post to seek election to the United States Senate from Illinois. He served in the upper house from 1849 to 1855, when Trumbull won the seat after the state legislature deadlocked between Shields and Lincoln. Douglas then appointed Shields as a land commissioner in Minnesota Territory, where he promoted Irish immigration to settle the region.

When Minnesota was admitted to the Union, Shields was elected United States senator from that state and served until 1859. Failing to be re-elected, he moved to San Francisco, married the daughter of an old Irish friend, and soon settled in Mazatlan, Mexico, where he managed a mining property. He returned to the United States when the Civil War erupted, and by August 18, 1861, he had been commissioned a brigadier general of United States Volunteers and had won some distinction in early campaigns in the Shenandoah Valley.

In 1863, Shields resigned his commission and returned to San Francisco, where he served as a state railroad commissioner until the end of the war. He then moved to Missouri and again became active in politics, but lost a disputed race for Congress in 1872. He served in the Missouri legislature and on the state railway commission, and was much in demand as a public speaker. In January, 1879, he was again elected to the United States Senate—surely the only man to serve in that body from three different states. He died in Ottumwa, Iowa, on June 1, 1879, while on a lecture tour. Illinois, Minnesota, and Missouri have honored him with statues.

Many of the other officers who gained fame in the Mexican War went on to notable careers. Among them was Major General Robert Patterson. He commanded a division at Cerro Gordo and led in the pursuit that resulted in the capture of Jalapa. Later, when Scott had no command commensurate with Patterson's rank, he was given the difficult task of keeping supplies and reinforcements moving from Veracruz to the Valley of Mexico.

In July, 1848, Patterson returned to his business interests which he expanded to include sugar and cotton plantations in Louisiana and a chain of cotton mills in Pennsylvania. He was also active in promoting railroad and steamship transportation serving Philadelphia. He was an original trustee of Lafayette College, at Easton, Pennsylvania, and for five years was president of the Board of Trustees of the college.

When the Civil War began, Patterson, though nearly seventy years old, was mustered into service for three months to command the military department that included Pennsylvania, Delaware, Maryland, and the District of Columbia. His active commission expired in July, 1861, but he continued to command a division of Pennsylvania Militia until 1867. His military career, begun in 1833, thus spanned thirty-four years. He died in 1881.

Patterson's only rival in length of military service was his commander in the Mexican War, Winfield Scott. When Patterson left active service, Scott was still commanding general of the United States Army, a command he had held for thirty years. Indeed, he had been a general since the War of 1812. Scott's many other achievements, as well as those of fellow Mexican War generals Zachary Taylor and Franklin Pierce, are too well known to warrant repeating them here. The later careers of less famous military leaders whose names appear in Tennery's diary may be of interest, however.

Colonel Charles Clark, who was in command of troops in Matamoros while Tennery was stationed there, was a former member of the Mississippi legislature, where he had served from 1838 to 1844. After the war he returned to his home state and in 1856 was again elected to the state legislature, though he failed to be elected to Congress in the same year, losing to the former regimental commander, Reuben Davis. He remained in the state legislature until 1861. Clark served as brigadier general in the Confederate army, was wounded at Shiloh, and was wounded again and permanently crippled at Baton Rouge. He was elected governor of Mississippi in 1862 and re-elected in 1864, defeating Reuben Davis, who had served as a major general in the Confederate army and later as a representative in the Confederate Congress. Following the war, Clark served as a district judge until his death in 1877.

Another colonel Tennery encountered along the Río Grande was Henry R. Jackson, commander of the disorderly Georgia regiment. Only twenty-six years old at the time, Jackson had graduated from Yale with honors at nineteen and at twenty-four was a United States district attorney. After the war he edited the *Savannah Georgian* for a time, and in 1849 was appointed a superior court judge. He resigned in 1853 to accept a post as chargé d'affaires in Austria (his father had once held a like post in Paris), and was later promoted to minister. Upon his return to the United States in 1858, he was offered the post of chancellor of the University of Georgia (where his father had long been a professor). He declined the offer and resumed the practice of law. He also dabbled in politics and in 1861 was appointed a Confederate judge in Georgia. He resigned to accept an appointment as brigadier general in the Confederate army, and was a major general of Georgia troops when Atlanta fell in 1864. He then served under Hood in Tennessee until he was captured by Union forces.

After the Civil War, Jackson returned to his law practice. He was very active in politics, though he sought no office for himself. He served as minister to Mexico under President Cleveland. For twenty-five years he was president of the Georgia Historical Society, and he was a trustee of the Peabody Education Fund. He was also the author of two volumes of poetry. He died in 1898.

Among the other generals whom Tennery encountered

were Worth, Wool, and Twiggs of the Regular Army and Quitman and Pillow of the Volunteers. Colonel William S. Harney is also referred to more than once. Like Baker, Shields, and Lane, each of these men left his mark on the expanding West.

General William J. Worth commanded the Department of Texas immediately after the Mexican War and died there of cholera in 1849. Fort Worth was named for him.

General John E. Wool, a native of New York, was presented a sword by his home state in recognition of his service in the war. He commanded the Eastern Military Division for five years after the war, and was then transferred to San Francisco, where as the commander of the Department of the Pacific he was responsible for suppressing Indian outbreaks in Oregon and Washington from 1854 to 1857. Thereafter he again commanded the Department of the East, saving Fortress Monroe at the start of the Civil War. As commander of the Department of Virginia, Wool was promoted to regular major general in May, 1862, and a year later was retired because of age—he was then eighty years old. He died in Troy, New York, five years later, leaving a sizable endowment to Rensselaer Polytechnic Institute. The large monument to his memory in Troy has an inscription by William Cullen Bryant.

General David E. Twiggs was in command of the Department of Texas in February, 1861, and surrendered to the Confederacy. He was appointed a major general in the Confederate army, but died in 1862.

General John A. Quitman returned to the political wars in Mississippi, served as governor from 1850 to 1852 and in the United States Congress from 1855 until his death in 1858.

General Gideon J. Pillow, whose chief distinction was

that he had once been Polk's law partner, returned to his practice in Tennessee and engaged in political intrigues. In 1852 he played a part in Franklin Pierce's nomination (as he had that of Polk in 1844), but in 1856 he failed to receive the nomination for vice president that he coveted. When Tennessee seceded from the Union, he was named the major general in charge of Tennessee troops and was later a brigadier general in the Confederate army. As one of the generals who surrendered Fort Donaldson to General Grant in 1862, Quitman was temporarily suspended from duty and never again held an important command. After the Civil War, he practiced law for a time in Memphis and died a few years later in Helena, Arkansas.

Colonel William S. Harney, Scott's cavalry commander, is mentioned by Tennery for his bravery at both Veracruz and Cerro Gordo. For the latter battle he was breveted brigadier general. Following the Mexican War, Harney fought the Sioux in the Platte River region and by 1858 was a regular brigadier commanding the Department of Oregon. It was he who seized San Juan Island and almost precipitated a war with Great Britain. In 1861 he was in St. Louis commanding the Department of the West. In this capacity he saw fit to arrive at a kind of truce with General Sterling Price agreeing not to attack the secessionist Missouri troops if Price did not move against the federal government. For this agreement he was relieved of his command and was finally retired in 1863. In 1865 he was breveted major general for his long and faithful service and lived quietly until his death in Orlando, Florida.

As every student of American history is aware, many of the famous military leaders of the Civil War gained their first combat experience in the Mexican War. Alfred Hoyt

Bill expressed it aptly in the title of his book on that war, calling it *Rehearsal for Conflict*. But as Tennery's diary reminds us, many obscure or half-forgotten men also played their roles in the building of the nation. Tennery has also given us a picture of the everyday life of a citizen soldier. He makes it clear that fighting is oftentimes the smallest part of soldiering and also that politics, politicians, and generals are not the only components of a war.

Appendix

News Report from *The Georgian*,
Monday, September 14, 1846

From the New Orleans Commercial Times, 7th Inst.

Terrible Riot—Loss of Life

A very melancholy affair, little creditable to the discipline, order, and character for civilization, which, in spite of all that has occurred during the present campaign, we are proud to say are the attributes of the volunteers, occurred near Bur[r]ita, Rio Grande, on the 31st inst. On that day a steamboat took on board at Burita, five companies of one of the Georgia regiments. A good deal of animosity had previously been exhibited by two of these companies one against another; one of the rivals was an Irish company. From some circumstances or other, not explained, a row broke out in the evening between them—close proximity, we presume, producing hostile collision—and firearms and bayonets and swords were very freely used. The Colonel of the Georgia regiment did all he could to put an end to this disgraceful affray, but so fierce was the conflict between the contending parties that all was unavailing, although it is stated he shot one man and wounded two more with his own hand. While the battle was raging between these insensates on the deck of the steamboat, Col. Baker, 4th Illinois regiment, ordered out companies A and G, commanded by Captains Roberts and Johns, to assist in putting an end to it. He then went forward at the head of twenty men and urged the rioters to desist, but on his attempting to ascend the ladder of the steamboat he was fiercely attacked by those on board, and after a desperate fight, in which he was shot through the neck, the ball entering behind and passing through his cheek, penetrating him at once, his small party was obliged to retreat, having no ammunition with them, carrying off Col. Baker senseless. Commissary Post, Sergeant Oglesby and six men of the Illinois regiment were wounded—two mortally. Captain Roberts, company A, then attempted to board the boat but, after a desperate conflict, he and his men were beaten off. Captain R[oberts] received a severe bayonet wound through the shoulder into the back, three inches in length.

The affair having now assumed a very serious aspect, Maj. Harris brought out the whole remaining force of the 4th Illinois regiment, well provided with ball cartridge. At sight of this, the rioters ceased their disturbance, when the Georgians were disarmed and placed under a strong guard. Col. Baker, who received his wound while fighting hand to hand with the Captain of the Irish company of the Georgia battalion (also severely hurt) will recover, it is said, as will also Capt. Rogers [Roberts]. There were thirty lying wounded on the boat and on shore, on the morning of the 1st inst. Those who were killed outright, some eight or ten, were said to have been thrown overboard. An inquiry was to have been immediately instituted to ascertain the causes of this sad affair. Next arrival will give us more details.

The Picayune of the 6th inst. says—"While the fight was

going on, the Colonel of the Georgia regiment endeavored most gallantly to quell it, interfering personally, and attacking the rioters with sword and pistol. He shot down one man and wounded several others. Finding that he could not succeed in putting an end to the disturbance, he called on Col. Baker of the 4th regiment of Illinois volunteers for assistance."

Bibliography

Bill, Alfred Hoyt. *Rehearsal for Conflict: The War with Mexico, 1846–1848.* New York, 1947.

Brooks, Nathan Covington. *A Complete History of the Mexican War: Its Causes, Conduct, and Consequences.* Chicago, 1965.

Claiborne, J. F. H. *Life and Correspondence of John A. Quitman.* 2 vols. New York, 1860.

Complete History of the Late Mexican War, Containing an Authentic Account of All the Battles Fought in the Republic, Including the Treaty of Peace, with a List of the Killed and Wounded, Together with a Brief Sketch of the Lives of Generals Scott and Taylor. New York, 1865.

Esposito, Colonel Vincent J., ed. *The West Point Atlas of American Wars.* New York, 1959.

Farber, George C. *The Twelve Month Volunteer.* Cincinnati, 1848.

Frost, John. *The Mexican War and Its Warriors.* New Haven, 1850.

Heitman, Frances B. *Historical Register and Dictionary of the United States Army.* 2 vols. Washington, 1903.

Henry, Robert Selph. *The Story of the Mexican War.* Indianapolis, 1950.

Lavender, David. *Climax at Buena Vista: The American*

Campaigns in Northeastern Mexico, 1846–47. Philadelphia, 1966.

Marshall, T. M. *A History of the Western Boundary of the Louisiana Purchase, 1819–1841*. Berkeley, 1914.

Nevins, Allan, ed. *Polk: The Diary of a President, 1845–1849, Covering the Mexican War, the Acquisition of Oregon and the Conquest of California and the Southwest*. New York, 1952.

Peterson, Clarence Stewart. *Known Military Dead During the Mexican War*. Baltimore, 1857.

Price, Glenn W. *Origins of the War with Mexico: The Polk-Stockton Intrigue*. Austin, 1967.

Rappaport, Armin. *The War with Mexico: Why Did It Happen?* Chicago, 1964.

Regimental and company rosters, Illinois State Archives.

Rives, G. L. *The United States and Mexico, 1821–1848*. 2 vols. New York, 1913.

Ruiz, Ramon Eduardo. *The Mexican War: Was It Manifest Destiny?* New York, 1963.

Singletary, Otis A. *The Mexican War*. Chicago, 1960.

Smith, Justin H. *The War with Mexico*. 2 vols. New York, 1919.

Index

Alamita Hacienda, Mexico: 58
Albany Convention: vii
Almonte, Juan: xiv
Altamira, Mexico: 60
Alton, Ill.: 4
American Revolution: vii
Amity, Ill.: 4
Amity and Commerce, Treaty of, (U.S.-Mexico, 1832): xii
Ampudia, Gen. Pedro de: xviii, xxv, xxvi; defends Monterrey, xxvii; asks for armistice, xxviii
Anaquitas, Mexico: xxv
Andonega, Fort (Mexico): 68
Arista, Gen. Mariano: xviii, xxv, xxvi
Armijo, Gov. Manuel: xxi
Artillery: American, xxvi, xxxii; American losses of, Mexicans at Veracruz, 72; American, at Cerro Gordo, 81; Mexican, at Cerro Gordo, 82

Baker, Col. Edward D.: xxxiii, 4, 13, 14, 18–20, 41, 65; reconnoiters Cerro Gordo, 79
Baton Rouge, La.: 95
Beason, William: 25
Beauregard, Lt. Peter G. T.: xxxii
Bebee, David: 36
Belford, Owen: 66
Belknap, Camp (Texas): xxvi
Billsboro, Henry: 85
Bennett, Corp. Martin: 16
Benton, Sen. Thomas Hart: xxix
Bernal, Mount (Mexico): 59
Big Hatchie (steamboat): 24, 27
Bite, Dr. (military doctor): 87
Boca Chica (Mexico): 13
Brazos Island (Mexico): xxv, 13, 24
Brown, Fort (Texas): xviii, xxv, 29
Brown, Maj. Jacob: 29, 42
Brownsville, Texas: 29
Buchanan, Secretary of State James: xiv
Buena Vista, Battle of: xxx, xxi, 72
Burrita, Mexico: 24, 41
Butler, Anthony: xii
Butler, Gen. William O.: 10, 11

Cadwalader, Gen. George: 11, 93
Cahuenga, Rancho (Mexico): xxii
Cairo, Ill.: 10, 96
Calhoun, Secretary of State John C.: xiv
California: xx
Camargo, Mexico: 27, 30, 32, 43, 44, 65
Carpentero, Lake (Mexico): 60
Cary, Samuel: 3

Cassidy, Dr. Alexander M.: 89
Cast, Archibald: 89
Cerro Gordo, Battle of: xxxii, 81–82
Chapultepec, Battle of: xxxiv
Chocoi Hacienda (Mexico): 58
Churchill, Col. Sylvester: xxiv, 8
Ciudad Victoria: *see* Victoria, Ciudad
Clark, Col. Charles: at Matamoros, xxviii; as commander of Second Mississippi Infantry, 29
Clifton, Job: 44
Clifton, William: 84
Colonel Cross (steamboat): 25
Conner, Com. David: xxx
Cook, Rev. John S.: viii
Cooke, Lt. Col. Philip St. George: xxi
Cornell, Samuel: 43, 55
Corvette (steamboat): 39
Cowardan, Lt. George W.: 81
Croghan, Col. George: 8
Cross, Trueman: 25

Davenport, Col. William: 6
Davenport, Corp. Isaiah: 83
Davenport, Sgt. Uriah: 85
Davis, Corp. William: 55
De la Vega, Gen. R. Díaz: 82, 83
Depew, James: 86
DeWitt County, Ill.: 5
Dillon, Charles W.: 16
Doniphan, Col. Alexander W.: xxi, xxii, xxiii, 96
Duck, John: 56

Eclipse (steamboat): 9, 11
Edgar County, Ill.: 15
Effingham County, Ill.: viii
El Telégrafo (hill): xxxiii

Farber, George C.: 10
Foreman, Col. Ferris: 10, 47
Forlón, Río: 57
Fourth Illinois Volunteers: at Cerro Gordo, xxxiii, xxxiv; on Río Grande, 10; on Brazos Island, 13
Freeman, Capt. James: 5
Frémont, Col. John C.: xx, xxi

Galveston (steamboat): 94
Georgia Regiment: 18–20, 60
Gillespie, Archibald: xx
Greenville, Ill.: 3
Guadalupe Hidalgo, Treaty of: xxxiv
Gulf of Mexico: 63

Hamilton, Sgt. Absalom: 83
Hancock (steamer): 95
Handchey, 1st Sgt. John M.: 81
Harney, Col. William S.: xxiv, xxxiii, 76
Harris, Maj. Thomas L.: 43, 47, 79
Henry, James: 3, 40
Hirt, Capt. John C.: 18, 32
Hite, Levi: 3, 24, 44, 61
Hodge, Andrew J.: 22
Howard, Lt. Benjamin: 27
Huntsville (steamboat): 96

Inman, James: 3, 17, 25, 35, 43
Isabel, Point (Texas): xxv, xxviii, 62
Iturbide, Emperor Augustin: 53

Jackson, Joshua E.: 82, 83
Jalapa, Mexico: 83, 84
Jefferson Barracks, Mo.: 6
Jenkins, James M.: 89
John Garrow (ship): 95
Johnson, Lt. Sheldon: 87

Johnson, Theophilus: 3, 17, 35
Jones, Capt. Edward: 19, 34, 80
Julian, Capt. Evan: 95

Kaskaskia River: 10
Kearny, Gen. Stephen Watts: xx, xxi, 77
Kenney, Ambrose: 36
Kinney, Corp. William: 43, 86, 89

La Atalaya (hill): xxxiii
Lee, Lt. Robert E.: xxxii
Lincoln, Pres. Abraham: vii
Lobos Islands: xxx
Lowry, Sgt. William: 43, 86, 93

McConkey, Capt. John S.: 11
McGarvey, Alex: 7
McGarvey, Henry: 65
McNeil, Lt. W. L.: 42
McNeil, Peter: 5
McPherson, Jesse L.: 16
McReynolds, H. C.: 11
Maltby, Lt. Charles: 85
Marcy, Secretary of War William L.: xv
Marine, Ill.: 4
Marshall, Gen. Humphrey: xxviii, 11
Mason, Capt. Stevens T.: 88
Matamoros, Mexico: xviii, xxv, 26, 31, 39, 40
Mejía, Gen. Francisco: xviii, xxvi, xxvii
Memphis, Tenn.: 96
Mexican War: unpopularity of, in United States, vii; events leading to, vii, ix; declaration of, xix
Mexico, Republic of: 38
Missouri (steamboat): 7
Missouri Mounted Volunteers: xxi, 95, 96
Molino del Rey, Battle of: xxxiv
Monterrey, Mexico: 34, 43
Moore, Lt. Col. John: 65
Mormon Battalion: xxi
Morris, Capt. Achilles: 67
Morris, William: 91
Murphy, Lt. Richard: 55

Nance, Willis T.: 33
Natchez, Miss.: 11
National Highway (Mexico): xxxi–xxxiv, 78
Naval Battery, U.S. (Battery No. 5): 74
Newcomb, Capt. Daniel: 5, 84
New Mexico: xx
New Orleans, La.: 10, 11, 95
New York Volunteer Regiment: xxxiv, 82

Oglesby, Lt. Richard J.: 18, 34, 44
Ohio River: 10
Orizaba, Mount: 86, 89, 93
Orleans (steamer): 70

Pacific Squadron, U.S.: xx
Page, Capt. John: 7
Palo Alto, Battle of: xxv
Paredes, Mexico: xxv, 27, 29
Patterson, Camp: 14, 22
Patterson, Gen. Robert: on Río Grande, xxviii, xxxii, 11, 43; battery of, 73; visits hospital, 85
Payne, Calvin: 22
Perote, Mexico: 92
Perry, Com. Matthew C.: xxxii
Perryman, James: 3, 25, 43, 44, 82
Pillow, Gen. Gideon J.: at Camargo, xxviii, 10, 11, 58; leads brigade at Cerro Gordo, 80

Plan del Río, Mexico: xxxii, 79, 82, 83
Plunkett, B.: 9
Poinsett, Joel Roberts: xii
Polk, Pres. James K.: vii
Post, Commissary Joel Seth: 20
Post, Lt. John F.: 61
Polto River (Mexico): 58

Quitman, Gen. John A.: xxviii, 10, 11, 43, 54; leads expedition to Alvarado, 76

Redd, Lt. Col. Thomas Y.: 20
Resaca de la Palma, Battle of: xxvi, 29
Reynosa, Mexico: 39
Richards, Isaac: 22
Riley, Col. Bennett: xxxiii
Río del Tigre: 44
Roberts, Capt. Horatio E.: 19, 34
Ross, Lt. Leonard F.: 56
Rudder, Thomas: 59, 60

Sacrificios Island: xxxi, 72
St. Louis, Mo.: 9, 96
Salem, Ill.: 96
San Antonio (stream): 52
San Fernando, Mexico: 43, 49
San Juan River: 33
Santa Anna, Gen. Antonio López de: xxvii, xxviii; threatens Saltillo, xxix, xxxi; at Cerro Gordo, xxxiii; in battle near Saltillo, 70; estates of, along National Highway, 78; hacienda of, 84
Santander, Mexico: 51
Santa Teresa, Mexico: 43
Sawyer, Pratt: 84
Scott, Gen. Winfield: xxix, 57, 79, 87
Sea Lion (steamboat): 11
Second Ohio Regiment: 95
Shelby County, Ill.: 5
Shelbyville, Ill.: 3
Shelton, Moses: 81
Sheron of Bath (ship): 70
Shields, Gen. James: xxiv; with Wool, xxiv, 11, 25, 43, 64, 67; reconnoiters Cerro Gordo, 79
Skidmore, Reuben: 38
Slidell, John: xviii
Sloat, Com. John D.: xx
Smith, Himelion: 21
Smith, Col. Persifor F.: xxxiii
Souther, Temple: 25
Spitfire (ship): 72
Stockton, Com. Robert F.: xx
Sultan (steamboat): 9

Tamaulipas, state of, Mexico: xxviii, xxix
Tampico, Mexico: xxx, 35, 42, 61, 68
Taylor, Gen. Zachary, elected president: vii; in Seminole War, xv; moves U.S. Army to Texas, xviii; at Palo Alto, xxv; at Resaca de la Palma, xxvi; captures Matamoros, xxvi; captures Monterrey, xxviii
Tennery, Thomas D.: early life of, viii; later life of, 99
Tennessee Cavalry Regiment: 10, 47, 92
Texas: American and Mexican claims to: ix, x; revolution and independence of, xi; admitted to the Union, xii; boundary dispute of, with Mexico, xii
Texas Rangers: 9
Third Regiment of Illinois Volunteers: 37, 42, 43
Thomas, William A.: 3
Thompson, Waddy: xiv
Thornby, Leroy: 82, 83, 91

Thornton, Capt. Seth B.: xviii
Thorp, Joseph: 84
Todd, James I. D.: 92
Tony (steamboat): 39
Torrejón, Gen. (Mexican officer): xxv
Troy (steamboat): 42
Twiggs, Gen. David E.: xxviii, xxxiii, xxxiv, 67, 77; encounters Mexican forces, 78; at battle of Cerro Gordo, 80, 82
Tyler, Pres. John: xi

Ulúa, Fortress San Juan de: xxi

Veracruz: Battle of, xxi, 67; sailing near, 71; traffic to and from, 83; capture of, 92; Tennery leaves, 94
Vicksburg, Miss.: 11, 96
Victoria, Ciudad: xxix, xxx, 43
Vinson, Sgt. John: 14, 84
Vinton, Capt. John Rogers: 73

Wallace, Lt. Andrew J.: 65
Wallace, William: 34
Wheat, Capt. Chatham R.: 75
Whig party: critical of Mexican War, vii; elects Zachary Taylor president, vii
Whillis, Isaac W.: 43
Whitesville (steamer): 41
Whiting, Capt. Daniel Powers: 89
Winter, Gilbert E.: 47
Wool, Gen. John: xxii–xxiv, 35
Worth, Gen. William J.: at Saltillo, xxiv; at Monterrey, xxvii, xxxiv, 77

Yan, Alonzo A.: 23

The paper on which this book is printed bears the watermark of the University of Oklahoma Press and has an effective life of at least three hundred years.